"FOR WE WALK BY FAITH, NOT BY SIGHT."
-2 CORINTHIANS 5:7

FAITH. PILGRIMAGE. REVIVAL

Series Preface: Inviting Revival

There is an epidemic plaguing the Western church. The Gospel of Jesus Christ is being trampled underfoot and not much is being done about it. What is more, those who have been entrusted with the task of shepherding souls have so denigrated, watered down, or over nuanced the grace of God that they have caused Jesus' sheep to falsely find their eternal security in a message that scarce represents the biblical gospel.

If any of this be true (and I believe it is), then it is not enough to sit idly by and hope for a better tomorrow. No, we must bloody our knees in prayer, soak our faces with tears, wet our pens with ink, and preach our throats raw in the hope that God would show our generation a supernatural grace that would revive our tepid faith. We must clarify not only the person and work of Jesus Christ, but the cost associated with following him.

In short, we need revival. We don't need forceful and clumsy emotionalism; vicious anti-intellectualism; or cold, dead orthodoxy— we need a Spirit-led, prayer-ignited movement of God. These resources attempt to serve that end. My prayer is that they would bring glory to God and spur your heart to pray for, and work toward, personal and corporate revival. It is with love that we labor to make Christ and his abrasive, yet life-giving gospel known. And it is with urgency that we plead with you to deal soberly with the deeper reality to which these resources point.

- **Brandon Scalf**
Founder and Director,
Dead Men

The
IMPLICATIONS
of
FAITH

by CRAIG MILLER

DM LITERATURE
RESOURCES FOR REVIVAL

for more information visit deadmenstuff.com

The Implications of Faith
DM Literature
Indianapolis, Indiana

Published in the United States in association with DM Literature, a division of Dead Men Ministries. www.deadmenstuff.com

ISBN-10: 0-578-41055-9
ISBN-13: 978-0-578-41055-5

Cover design: John Pyle (https://pyle.design)
Instagram: @pyledesign

10 9 8 7 6 5 4

To Brittany,
my beautiful wife, biggest supporter,
and best friend

CONTENTS

PROLOGUE

All is not well.

Pardon me if I sound dramatic. I do not intend to be more so than I need to be, but I find there is cause for great concern with the current state of Christianity—particularly in the West. I believe it to be very ill.

Most concerning, perhaps, with the type of illness I am speaking of, is that the one who is ill often times thinks himself to be completely healthy.

Imagine with me, if you will, that you have found yourself in the most dire of life-threatening situations. Time is running out if you hope to survive; you must act quickly. Now imagine you are in correspondence via radio transmission with the Chief of Intelligence, who is giving you step-by-step instructions on what you must do to survive. As he approaches the end of the instructions, he carefully explains, "And most importantly, if you want to survive, all you have to do is...[static]."

Just as he is stating the most important part of the instructions, the reception on the radio breaks up. Frantically, you ask him to repeat the last part—the important part. "If you want to survive, all you have to do is...[static]." Again, the signal breaks up; only this time, transmission is lost completely. Time is running out, and you're missing the most important part of the instructions. You would be in grave danger *and* you would be aware of it, right?

Now imagine the signal didn't break up, and you clearly heard and understood the instructions. You would feel a lot better, correct? As long as you follow the instructions, all is good. You needn't worry.

But there is a third scenario, and I think this appropriately explains our current situation. What if you heard the words of instruction clearly and believed you understood them, but the Chief of Intelligence actually meant something different by his words from what you thought he meant? You would be in grave danger, but you would think yourself safe, would you not?

It is not enough to possess the right instructions; we must also have a right understanding of those instructions. Words matter—more specifically, the meaning of words matter, perhaps none more so regarding our current spiritual state within the church than the meaning of the word *faith*. Instead of allowing God to define his own terms through the Bible, we have projected our own understanding of the word *faith* onto the Scriptures. Consequently, we feel secure in our salvation, when I fear the truth for many of us is that it is a false security. Spiritually, we remain quite ill, and yet we think ourselves healthy.

I am nobody special. I don't have a large following or a household name. I have no fame or fortune to speak of, and I have never written a book before this one. While I do have a modest amount of seminary training, I am a Personal Trainer by trade. I serve my local church only in a lay capacity. In nearly every respect, my life has been ordinary, except for one: I have experienced spiritual revival to a degree that I have come to realize is entirely extraordinary.

Ten years ago, the Lord rescued me from the grips of spiritual apathy and indifference—from a lukewarm, "cultural Christianity"—

and set my soul ablaze with a fire and fervor that I can scarcely put into words. He did so by deconstructing and reconstructing my entire understanding of what it means to follow Jesus in faith.

This book is the result of that process.

It has not been an easy road. Passion and fire do not always equal fun and happiness; quite the opposite, in fact. The journey of faith has led me to places I would have never chosen for myself to go. Spiritual growth requires another type of fire: the fire of trials and tribulations (the refiner's fire), meant to test us, mold us, shape us, grow us, and prove our faith to be genuine and our salvation secure.

Nevertheless, if you do choose to embark upon the journey of faith, I promise that you will find Jesus far superior to the lesser meddlings of this life—that the fire and fervor that come from a revived and renewed Spirit far outweigh the fleeting triviality of any momentary comfort or pleasure this world could offer.

I have written this book because I believe I am not alone in the spiritual apathy, indifference, and lukewarm, "cultural Christianity" that had come to define my spiritual state. As you read, I pray that you too will allow the Holy Spirit to challenge your preconceptions of *faith*, and in doing so, he will set your soul ablaze like he did mine, with a fire and a fervor for Jesus like you have never known before.

Fire

"God of Abraham, God of Isaac, God of Jacob,"
not of philosophers and scholars.
Certainty, certainty, heartfelt, joy, peace.
God of Jesus Christ,
My God and Your God.
"Your God shall be my God."

The world forgotten, and everything except God.
He can only be found by the ways taught in the Gospels.
Greatness of the human soul.

"O righteous father, the world had not known thee,
but I have known thee."
Joy, joy, joy, tears of joy.

-Blaise Pascal, November 23, 1654
(following his own experience with spiritual revival)

INTRODUCTION

Little Danny stood at the edge of the swimming pool and stared into the sparkly blue abyss. He was excited and yet scared; he knew the prospect of joy to be had in the pool. He'd seen the other children splashing about, laughing and shrieking in pure delight. He wanted to learn how to swim, and yet, a fear gripped him—a fear of the unknown. "What if the water's too cold? What if I can't do it? What if I sink? What if I get hurt or choke on the water?"

Just then, Danny's dad walked up beside him and put his arm around his boy. "Are you ready to do this, little man?" he asked.

"Yes…I think so," Danny warily replied.

As his dad calmly entered the water, he smiled, extended his arms, and beckoned his boy, "Jump! I'll catch you!"

But Danny didn't move. He just stood there, staring at his dad—frozen by fear.

"Jump!" his dad urged again.

Again, Danny just stood there like a deer caught in the headlights. He didn't move.

This time, his dad moved a little bit closer—arms still extended. "Do you trust me, buddy?"

Danny nodded his head affirmatively.

"Then jump!"

Danny paused…and then shook his head "no."

One more time, his dad asked, "Do you trust me?"

Again, Danny nodded his head up and down.

"Then jump, buddy. I love you, and I promise I will catch you."

What Danny does next will be very telling. Does he really trust his dad? He says he does. He thinks he does. But if it doesn't result in an action that reflects that supposed trust, does he really trust him? If he really believed that his dad loved him, had his best interest in mind, and was capable of catching him, wouldn't he jump?

We have used the word *faith*—a word that is active— interchangeably with *mere belief.* Our understanding of *mere belief* is "to ascend to certain intellectual truths." This form of belief is capable of existing entirely in the ethereal realm, disconnected from any real application of its truths. It is capable of existing there for quite some time before it causes us to move, act, or change (if it ever does). We say, "Let my faith grow a little more and then I will act; then I will jump. But until then, I am saved by my belief."

We have come to believe that faith and action can be separated— that mere belief in the precepts of the Christian faith (namely the Gospel message) is all that is required for us to be saved. For many of us, this understanding of grace has become a warm blanket assuring us of eternal life. We hear John 3:16 ("For God so loved the world, that he gave his only Son, that whoever believes in him should not perish but have eternal life") and Ephesians 2:8 ("For by grace you have been saved through faith") and we project this understanding of faith onto such verses. But what if we have misunderstood? What if God is saying through these verses something different than what we think he is saying? What if faith is more than mere belief?

To address this point, James 2:14-16 says, "What good is it, my brothers, if someone says he has faith but does not have works? Can that faith save him? If a brother or sister is poorly clothed and lacking in daily food, and one of you says to them, 'Go in peace, be warmed and filled,' without giving them the things needed for the body, what good is that?"

James is so eloquently explaining that if there is a logical disconnect between our words and our actions, then our words are meaningless. If we say to someone, "I care for you very much, and I see that you do not have much food or clothing," but we send that person away with well wishes that he be warm and filled, without feeding or clothing him ourselves, we do not actually care for him the way we claim. He concludes in 2:17, "So also faith by itself, if it does not have works, is dead."

James 2:21-24 (NLT, emphasis added) continues: "Don't you remember that our ancestor Abraham was shown to be right with God by his actions when he offered his son Isaac on the altar? You see, his faith and his actions worked together. *His actions made his faith complete.* And so it happened just as the Scriptures say: 'Abraham believed God, and God counted him as righteous because of his faith.'"

Faith, as the Bible defines it, is not mere intellectual belief; rather, *faith is the belief in a "truth" that is then made manifest in action.* Faith is trust and hope that evidences itself in the way we live our lives. Faith is acting apart from the way we are naturally inclined to act because we believe that what we claim to believe is actually true. It is little Danny standing on the edge of the pool and saying, "I'm scared to jump, but I trust my dad's love for me, so I will jump anyway."

This is faith.

Faith implies that our lives will make evident what we believe and who we believe in. For those of us who believe in Christ, faith implies that we will embark upon the journey of Christian discipleship (following Jesus), beginning with conversion and lasting until our death or Jesus' return. But this is no minor endeavor. For although grace is a gift freely offered to all who would believe, this grace is not cheap—and belief is not without cost.

As for mere belief, this is nothing short of the "faith" of demons. James 2:19 (NLT) contends, "You say you have faith, for you believe that there is one God. Good for you! Even the demons believe this, and they tremble in terror." Belief without the action of faith is of no more value to us than it is to the demons. Mere belief will not save us.

Jesus makes this clear in Matthew 7:21-23: "Not everyone who says to me, 'Lord, Lord,' will enter the kingdom of heaven, but the one who does the will of my Father who is in heaven. On that day many will say to me, 'Lord, Lord... And then will I declare to them, 'I never knew you; depart from me, you workers of lawlessness.'"

Dietrich Bonhoeffer adds:

> Having laid hold of cheap grace (mere belief as the means to salvation), they were barred forever from the knowledge of costly grace. Deceived and weakened, men felt that they were strong now that they were in possession of this cheap grace—whereas they had in fact lost the power to live the life of discipleship and obedience. The word of cheap grace has been the ruin of more Christians than any commandments of works.[1]

Our actions become the great revealer of what we actually believe. To profess faith in Christ but not live as if we trust him and his word is a logical disconnect—one that has great consequences both now and in eternity. This is why James 1:22 instructs, "Be doers of the word, and not hearers only, deceiving yourselves." Our lives ought to make evident the faith we claim to have—not perfectly but pervasively.

To be sure, I am not contending that we ought to try to earn God's love and forgiveness through our actions. We do not obey so that we will be saved. But rather, the evidences of faith (obedience not withstanding) are the natural, even necessary, outpourings of genuine faith and authentic Christianity.

In Matthew 7:17-20, Jesus says, "So, every healthy tree bears good fruit, but the diseased tree bears bad fruit. A healthy tree cannot bear bad fruit, nor can a diseased tree bear good fruit. Every tree that does not bear good fruit is cut down and thrown into the fire. Thus you will recognize them by their fruits."

If our life isn't producing evidence of what we claim to believe—good fruit as Jesus calls it—then we must conclude we are a diseased tree, still unconverted by genuine faith in the Gospel message.

1 John 2:2-6 is even more clear on this:

> He is the propitiation for our sins... And by this we know that we have come to know him, if we keep his commandments. Whoever says "I know him" but does not keep his commandments is a liar, and the truth is not in him, but whoever keeps his word, in him truly the love of God is perfected. By this we may know that we are in him: whoever says he abides in him ought to walk in the same way in which he walked.

Finally, in Ezekiel 36:26-27 (emphasis added), 600 years before Jesus would ever walk the earth and the Gospel was nothing more than a distant prophecy, it was written: "And I will give you a new heart, and a new spirit I will put within you. And I will remove the heart of stone from your flesh and give you a heart of flesh. And I will put my Spirit within you, *and cause you to walk in my statutes and be careful to obey my rules.*"

It was always intended that faith would work itself out through good deeds—through obedience to the Lord. It was always that grace would empower our pursuit of holiness, not excuse it. As Charles Spurgeon explains, "Grace is the mother and nurse of holiness. Not the apologist for sin."[2]

Christian, do you really believe what you claim to believe? Is your faith genuine? If your answer to both is a resounding "Yes," how then should you live?

2 Corinthians 13:5-6 urges us: "Examine yourselves, to see whether you are in the faith. Test yourselves. Or do you not realize this about yourselves, that Jesus Christ is in you?—unless indeed you fail to meet the test!"

My prayer is that this book would serve as a test for you as it seeks to explore the deep, life-altering implications of becoming a follower of Jesus Christ. I pray that it will challenge your preconceptions about grace and faith, and that you will see the free gift of grace as an invitation to *follow* Jesus, and not merely to ascend to an intellectual belief in his name. I pray that it would serve as a guide, lovingly walking you through what it means to embrace a theology of costly grace—of Biblical grace. Finally, it is my prayer that this book will lead you to a deeper love for Jesus that gives birth to the appropriate response to such grace.

This is not a book about doing better and trying harder. It is not a book about picking yourself up by your bootstraps and becoming a "better" Christian. It *is,* however, a book about surrendering more fully and being transformed more completely, pursuing Christ more intently and walking out your faith more radically. It is not a checklist of behaviors; discipleship is deeper than that. Rather, this book is an invitation to embark upon a journey to holistically (albeit not exhaustively) answer this question: What does it mean to follow Jesus in faith?

INTRODUCTION NOTES

[1] THE COST OF DISCIPLESHIP by Dietrich Bonhoeffer, translated from the German by R.H. Fuller, with revisions by Irmgard Booth. Copyright © 1959 by SCM Press Ltd. Reprinted with the permission of Scribner, a division of Simon & Schuster, Inc. All rights reserved. (Touchstone, New York, 1995), Kindle edition, 638.

[2] Taken from *Morning and Evening* by Charles Spurgeon, © 2003, Kindle edition, loc. 1210. Used by permission of Crossway, a publishing ministry of Good News Publishers, Wheaton, IL 60187, www.crossway.org."

ENTER BY THE NARROW GATE.
FOR THE GATE IS WIDE AND THE WAY IS EASY THAT
LEADS TO DESTRUCTION,
AND THOSE WHO ENTER BY IT ARE MANY.
FOR THE GATE IS NARROW AND THE WAY IS HARD
THAT LEADS TO LIFE,
AND THOSE WHO FIND IT ARE FEW.

— MATTHEW 7:13-14

PART I:
THE FOUNDATION
OF FAITH

Before you build a house, you have to lay a proper foundation. Without it, the house will not stand; it will not last. At the first sign of adverse conditions, the house will crumble. In the same way, before we talk about the implications of our faith—about faith manifesting itself in the way we live our lives—we must first lay the proper foundation.

Faith has an origin; it has a predecessor. Without the Gospel and God's grace there is no faith. Without Jesus, we have no hope. So before we continue with any conversation about faith, we have to start with the only true foundation. Before we continue on this journey, we have to understand grace (what it is *and* what it isn't), or we're going to get lost before we even get started.

I.

Grace: The Foundation of Faith

In the beginning, God created the heavens and the earth. He created the sun and the stars, the moon and the clouds, the oceans and the land. He created the plants and the trees, the birds of the air, and all the creatures of the land and sea. He looked at all that he created and declared it "good."

Then, God created man. He made him in his own likeness—the "Imago Dei" (the image of God). He placed man (Adam) in the Garden of Eden and assigned him the task of naming and caring for the animals. But something was missing. God declared it not good for man to be alone, so he fashioned a suitable helper—a wife—for Adam out of his rib (Woman = out of man). She was called Eve. And once again, God declared things to be good.

Mankind was intended to reflect God's glory to the rest of creation as its corporate head and God's ambassador, and to enjoy God and his creation forevermore. There was but one restriction: Adam and Eve were forbidden to eat the fruit from the tree of the knowledge of good and evil, or they would die (spiritual death leading to an eventual physical death).

Now the Serpent was crafty and deceitful, and knowing God's commandment, he set about to cause Adam and Eve to sin. He enticed and deceived Eve into eating the forbidden fruit, and she shared some with her husband Adam. From that point on, nothing was ever the same.

It is hard to put into words the magnitude of mankind's rebellion on that fateful day, as well as the catastrophic effects it unleashed on all creation. But, suffice to say, creation as God intended it—literal paradise as man experienced unadulterated relationship and intimacy with God—was lost.

We were created by God, for God, and to be in an intimate relationship with God—to know him. At this the Psalmist marveled: "When I look at your heavens, the work of your fingers, the moon and the stars, which you have set in place, what is man that you are mindful of him, and the son of man that you care for him? Yet you have made him a little lower than the heavenly beings and crowned him with glory and honor" (Psalm 8:3-5).

But, despite this divine purpose, we sold our birthright—the right to be sons and daughters of the most-high God. We traded it for self-autonomy and immediate gratification. We traded it for sin, which in its very nature, is a rejection of our God-given identity. It is a rejection of God himself and rebellion against his rightful role in our life—his position of Creator, Lord, and King.

In doing so, we severed the relationship. We broke the covenant bond and created a chasm between God and us—a chasm of insurmountable and irreversible distance. With our sin-infected hearts, we hated God, wanting nothing to do with Him or His will for our lives; having no desire to seek him or restore that relationship. But even if we would have had that desire, it wouldn't have mattered. He is holy; we were sin stained, unclean, and unworthy. What does the darkness have to do with the light? If one offense against a holy God is deserving of death, what does it matter if we perform a thousand good deeds in its wake?

But we were not just guilty of one offense. Our sins were too many to be numbered. We broke every commandment. We invented new ways of doing evil. Our very nature was rotten to the core, so rotten that we began to think our ways were not rotten. We began to think of ourselves as good! Yes, truly we stood condemned to die, justice demanding it so. We were every bit deserving of that fate: eternal separation from God (physical and spiritual death).

We are sinners deserving of hell—every last one of us. But this is not the message of our culture or our day. In fact, it is quite offensive to suggest it, for the message of our day is that people are inherently good. We are not sinners. We are not evil. We are not prideful, selfish, and hard-hearted. We don't need a Savior. We need freedom and space for our innate goodness to develop and prosper. We need positive re-enforcement and self-esteem so that we will know and believe in our "goodness." And regardless of what we think and desire, it ought to be celebrated because it only overflows from the goodness within us.

We have relegated morality to a subjective judgment, and we have made ourselves the judge. We justify our own worst actions while judging ourselves according to our best intentions. Meanwhile, we compare ourselves to the worst actions of those around us. This becomes the measure we use to determine our own "goodness." And just like that, we have built an airtight defense of our own righteousness.

But, if we're really honest with ourselves, we know it's not true; we know we are not righteous.

Have you ever met someone you believe is such a great person that just being around him or her makes you aware of your own shortcomings? How much more do you think we would be aware of our own sinfulness if we were in the presence of God himself—a God who is perfectly righteous and holy?

Peter is confronted with this exact scenario in Luke 5:1-8. As his eyes are opened to who Jesus really is, he is instantly made aware of his own sinfulness. The passage reads:

> On one occasion, while the crowd was pressing in on him to hear the word of God, he was standing by the lake of Gennesaret, and he saw two boats by the lake, but the fishermen had gone out of them and were washing their nets. Getting into one of the boats, which was Simon's, he asked him to put out a little from the land. And he sat down and taught the people from the boat. And when he had finished speaking, he said to Simon, "Put out into the deep and let down your nets for a catch." And Simon answered, "Master, we toiled all night and took nothing! But at your word I will let down the nets." And when they had done this, they enclosed a large number of fish, and their nets were breaking. They signaled to their partners in the other boat to come and help them. And they came and filled both the boats, so that they began to sink. But when Simon Peter saw it, he fell down at Jesus' knees, saying, "Depart from me, for I am a sinful man, O Lord."

We don't get to be the judge of our own "goodness," nor do we get to use the people around us as the measure by which we make the judgment. God and his holiness are the measure. He is the standard by which we are to be judged. God himself is the judge, and not one of us passes the test; not one of us measures up. We have *all* sinned, and we *all* fall short of the glory of God (Romans 3:23). Romans 6:23 tells us that the sentence for this—the payment required for sin—is death.

Every single one of us is dead and dying. We once were spiritual, united with the source of life (God himself). But our sin has separated us so that we are spiritually dead. Without connection to the source of life, our bodies are slowly wasting away, moving daily toward the same end as our spiritual selves.

We are like cell phones that have been disconnected from their chargers; our cords have been severed, our charge-ports damaged beyond repair. All that is left is the charge from when we used to be connected to a power outlet. With each passing moment, the charge weakens until it is no more.

In the same way, with each passing day we move closer to physical death, where we will stand before the holy, righteous, and just Judge and be forced to answer for our sin (the rejection and rebellion of God and His commandments). Here the finality of our physical and spiritual death will be realized, as we are sentenced to that which we have chosen, even desired, all along: eternity separated from God. Hell and its torments await, and we are every bit deserving of that fate.

This should be our fate. This *would* be our fate—every one of us—but for the grace of God.

The Gospel of Grace

You didn't save yourself. Did you know that?

The Bible explains that we were dead in our sins, and that something dead cannot choose God; it cannot bring itself back to life. This means that, left to ourselves, we are without hope. We cannot save ourselves.

There is no striving, no law abiding, and no elite cause to join that will be good enough to repay God for removing him from his throne (sin undermines the "god-ness" of God). In fact, Isaiah 64:6 says, "We have all become like one who is unclean, and all our righteous deeds are like a polluted garment. We all fade like a leaf, and our iniquities, like the wind, take us away." Another way to translate the Hebrew word for *polluted garment* is "used menstrual rag." Isaiah is emphasizing that because our hearts are so corrupted by sin, even our "righteous deeds" are filthy and unclean. Bryan Chapell explains, "God wants us to understand the true malignancy of our sin—the problem is too severe to be remedied by our goodness."[3]

We must understand this. We must grasp the magnitude of our sin and the futility of our own efforts to rectify the situation. Good works cannot save us. Not one of us will make it to heaven for being a "good person." We need a Savior, and the good news of the Gospel is that this is precisely what we have been given in Jesus.

The story of Christianity is a story of grace. It is a story about how an ill and undeserving people are again brought into a real and lasting relationship with the Creator of the universe, restoring us to true humanity. It is a story about us getting what we *don't* deserve. It is the story of how an eternal, transcendent, holy, and personal God came on a rescue mission as the God-man Jesus to die as a substitute for sinners—how he lived the life we could not live; died the death we should have died; and on the third day, rose from the dead and kicked open the tomb—conquering triumphantly over Satan, sin, death, and hell.

But why would he do this? Why would Jesus *willfully* die one of the most horrific deaths imaginable on the cross, *especially if he was God*?

The simple and yet remarkably profound answer ought to rattle us to the core: love. Jesus took on the cross out of love.

As undeserving as we might feel (and be), God loves us. He always has. As the Psalmist proclaims, "For you formed my inward parts; you knitted me together in my mother's womb. I praise you, for I am fearfully and wonderfully made" (Psalm 139:13-14). He loves us and doesn't want us to perish (2 Peter 3:9). In spite of our absolute rejection of him, he still wants us to have a relationship with him; he wants to redeem us.

But God is also holy and righteous. Sin has no part in him or with him. God, in his righteousness, is sincerely and exceedingly concerned about justice. This is why he must wage war against sin. Deuteronomy 32:4 explains, "The Rock, his work is perfect, for all his ways are justice. A God of faithfulness and without iniquity, just and upright is he."

God, therefore, executed the only plausible plan that could satisfy both his just nature and his lovingkindness; the only plan that could save us and yet judge sin. It was the only plan that could set us free from sin's control over us. *He* became the sacrifice. *He* became the substitute: "For our sake he [God] made him [Jesus] to be sin who knew no sin, so that in him we might become the righteousness of God" (2 Corinthians 5:21).

It is the purest expression of love the world has ever seen. Romans 5:8 explains, "God shows his love for us in that while we were still sinners, Christ died for us." 1 John 4:9-10 adds, "In this the love of God was made manifest among us, that God sent his only Son into the world, so that we might live through him. In this is love, not that we have loved God but that he loved us and sent his Son to be the propitiation for our sins."

Theologians have called this "the Great Exchange." The Bible calls it "grace."

There is, perhaps, not a more vivid and powerful depiction of this Great Exchange than in Donald Macleod's *The Person of Christ*. So that we might fully grasp the weight of that which Jesus took on in our stead, I will allow Macleod's words to speak for themselves:

> When Moses saw the glory of God on Mount Sinai so terrifying was the sight that he trembled with fear (Hebrews 12:21). But that was God in covenant: God in grace. What Christ saw in Gethsemane was God with sword raised (Zechariah 13:7; Matthew 26:31). The sight was unbearable. In a few short hours, he...would stand before that God answering for the sin of the world; indeed, identified with the

sin of the world (2 Corinthians 5:21). He became, as Luther said, "the greatest sinner that ever was" (Galatians 3:13). Consequently, to quote Luther again, "No one ever feared death so much as this man." He feared it because for him it was no sleep (1 Thessalonians 4:13), but the wages of sin: death with the sting; death unmodified and unmitigated; death as involving all that sin deserved. He alone would face it without a "covering," providing by his very dying the only covering for the world, but doing so as a holocaust, totally exposed to God's abhorrence of sin. And he would face death without God...deprived of the one solace and the one resource which had always been there....

...Even in Gethsemane, Jesus had been able to say, "Abba!" (term of endearment for Father). But now the cry is, "Eloi, Eloi" (my God, my God). He is aware only of the god-ness and power and holiness and otherness of God. In his self-image, he is no longer Son, but Sin; no longer...the Beloved with whom God is well-pleased, but...the *cursed one*: vile, foul, and repulsive....

... No grace was extended to him, no favour shown, no comfort administered, no concession made. God was present only as displeased, expressing that displeasure with overwhelming force in all the circumstances of Calvary.... He was cursed (Galatians 3:13), because he became the greatest thief, murderer, adulterer, robber, desecrator, blasphemer, etc., there has ever been anywhere in the world.

The paradox should not escape us. He was sinless. He was the Son of God. But there, on Golgotha, he was a sinner. He was sin (2 Corinthians 5:21)...damned and banished with the effect, as Calvin describes it, that "he must...grapple...with the armies of hell and the dread of everlasting death...suffering in his soul the terrible torments of a condemned and forsaken man." He was the scapegoat. He was "outside," in the outer darkness. He was beyond the cosmos, the realm of order and beauty, sinking instead into a black hole which no light could penetrate and from which, in itself, nothing benign or meaningful could ever emanate....

The gospel...is not that Christ shares our forsakenness but that he saves us from it. He endured it, not *with* us, but *for* us. We are immune to the curse (Galatians 3:13) and to the condemnation (Romans 8:3) precisely because Christ took them upon himself and went in our place, into the outer darkness.[4]

God came down in the person of Christ and bridged the chasm we created. We rejected him, hated him even, and yet he came after us. When we wanted nothing to do with him, he gave us a new heart and called us to himself. He saved us by showering us with grace upon grace. In this divine narrative, the hero dies for the villain. The judge is the one who is judged. The Son of God steps down from His throne to die in the place of the lowly sinner.

Jesus became the propitiation for our justification. That is, Jesus became our substitute by bearing our sins (past, present, and future) on a cross and receiving the just penalty we deserved for those sins. In doing so, we have been justified before God, meaning we have been restored to right standing in our relationship with Him. Our sins are no longer counted against us. Once again we can be sons and daughters of God. And it is offered to *all who would believe*: "Yet to all who did receive him, to those who believed in his name, he gave the right to become children of God—children born not of natural descent, nor of human decision or a husband's will, but born of God" (John 1:12-13, NIV).

This is grace.

* * * * *

You didn't save yourself.

Jonathan Edwards has been credited with surmising, "You contribute nothing to your salvation except the sin that made it necessary."[5] If you're a Christian—that is, if you've been purchased by the blood of Jesus for his glory—then you are a recipient of life-giving grace. You didn't struggle and strive your way back to God's favor by completing a checklist of works and good deeds, nor did you decide one day to wrap your arms around a soft and winsome philosopher who promised you a pleasant stay in the afterlife. You were, in love, ripped from the precipice of hell by a bloody, beaten, and broken Savior. And that is pure, unadulterated grace.

Joseph Ryan explains:

> Grace? What is grace? Is it a sprinkling of fairy dust, a warm happy feeling? No. Grace is a power that lifts you out of the domain of darkness and transfers you to the domain of light. Grace is God's magnificent power erupting in your heart and soul by his own intervention so that you move from death to life, from darkness to light, from hell to heaven. Grace is power that is embodied in a person.... Grace *is* a person...Jesus, come to you in the flesh.[6]

Jesus is the object of our faith. If we place our faith in anything else—any other person, idea, or construct of God we might have, then we've missed it. We might be religious or spiritual, moral, and ethical, but if it's not all about Jesus and his amazing grace for us, then we're still dead in our sins. As Acts 4:12 (NIV) reads, "Salvation is found in no one else, for there is no other name under heaven given to mankind by which we must be saved." Jesus *is* the Gospel (translated "good news").

In many ways, the journey on which we are about to embark will be a painful one. The road will be wearisome, the weather will be harsh, and the nights will be lonely. The *real* Gospel of Jesus Christ is abrasive at times. It is disorienting, and it is intense. If you are really seeing the Gospel for what it is, if you really get close, it's going to upset you, convict you, and transform you. But whatever you grasp from my words from this point on, I need you to tuck this nugget in your knapsack, for it will sustain you when your strength begins to decline:

> *Grace always precedes faith and it always fans into flame the faith that wanes as the harshness of this world beats it down.*

Grace is foundational. It is of first importance. It is the framework on which the rest of this book exists.

> And you were dead in the trespasses and sins in which you once walked, following the course of this world...and were by nature children of wrath, like the rest of mankind. But God, being rich in mercy, because of the great love with which he loved us, even when we were dead in our trespasses, made us alive together with Christ—*by grace you have been saved*—and raised us up with him and seated us with him in the heavenly places in Christ Jesus, so that in the coming ages he might show the immeasurable riches of his grace in kindness toward us in Christ Jesus. For by grace you have been saved through faith. *And this is not your own doing; it is the gift of God, not a result of works, so that no one may boast.*
>
> -Ephesians 2:1-9 (emphasis added)

CHAPTER 1 NOTES

[3] Taken from *Holiness by Grace* by Bryan Chapell, © 2001, p. 78. Used by permission of Crossway, a publishing ministry of Good News Publishers, Wheaton, IL 60187, www.crossway.org."

[4] Donald Macleod, *The Person of Christ*, (InterVarsity Press, Downers Grove, 1998), 174-178. Used by permission from InterVarsity Press UK.

[5] It is unclear if Edwards actually said this, but it is popularly attributed to him.

[6] Joseph F. Ryan, *That You May Believe: New Life in the Son*, (Crossway, Wheaton, 2003), 50-51. Used by Permission from Author.

II.

LIVING IN THE TENSION

There is another matter we must tend to before moving forward on this journey. It is a prerequisite, for apart from an understanding of the following, I fear the rest of the book will be in vain.

I love the simplicity of Christianity. I appreciate that Jesus didn't just choose the cultural elite and the academically gifted to be his disciples. Instead, he largely chose the simple and "uneducated" blue-collar workers like the fishermen and tax collectors. These were to be the ones who would be entrusted with taking the Gospel message to the ends of the earth.

Don't get me wrong; there is more than enough complexity in God to keep even the brightest of minds scratching their heads. But the basic tenets of the Gospel are simple enough that even a child can understand. This is why Paul, despite being an educated man, professes, "And I, when I came to you, brothers, I did not come proclaiming to you the testimony of God with lofty speech or wisdom. For I decided to know nothing among you except Jesus Christ and him crucified" (1 Corinthians 2:1-2).

We see the simplicity of Paul's message in Acts 16. Here, Paul and Silas have been imprisoned for preaching the Gospel. Around midnight, as Paul and Silas are praying and singing hymns, a great earthquake comes upon the jail and all the prison cells and shackles are shook loose. This leads to an incredible ministry opportunity for Paul and Silas to share the Gospel with the jailer keeping watch. In Acts 16:30-31 the jailer asks, "Sirs, what must I do to be saved?" to which Paul and Silas simply respond, "Believe in the Lord Jesus, and you will be saved, you and your household."

Similarly, in Acts 2, after Peter shows the crowd that they have murdered the Son of God, they ask what they must do to be saved. Acts 2:37-38 explains, "Now when they heard this they were cut to the heart, and said to Peter and the rest of the apostles, 'Brothers, what shall we do?' And Peter said to them, 'Repent and be baptized every one of you in the name of Jesus Christ for the forgiveness of your sins, and you will receive the gift of the Holy Spirit.'"

That is simple enough, right? Jesus crucified for our sins *is* the Gospel; to be saved all we must do is believe in the Lord Jesus, repent, and be baptized!

So, if it is so simple, why does it often seem complex? Why is there so much discord and division over doctrine? Why do we seem to either undershoot or overshoot a Biblical understanding of grace? How have we bastardized something so "simple"?

I believe the answer lies not in the complexity of the Gospel message, but in the complexity of the sin-marred lens through which we seek to understand that message. Sin is an intruder that ravages everything it touches. It has infected and affected our entire being. Every part of us and our faculties have been corrupted by sin. Thus, as we interpret and analyze everything through the lens of our sin (and our feelings, our wounds, our story, and even our personality types), we end up bringing all sorts of assumptions and preconceptions into the conversation. What should be simple is suddenly complex as we distort the simplicity to accommodate our sin-stained biases. What was once simple becomes complicated.

Have you ever taken a personality test? The first time I took one was while I was in seminary. For one of our classes, we were asked to take the Myers-Briggs personality assessment. The idea is that by answering 100 or so questions about ourselves, our basic temperaments and how we relate to the world around us can be determined. The test can tell if we are thinkers or feelers, extroverts or introverts, impulsive, planners, etc.

While I have more than a few issues with putting too much weight on these assessments, they can be very helpful in this particular conversation. I have found that, based on how a person is "wired," he will draw out and place extra emphasis on particular parts of Biblical truth. Those who are predominantly "feelers," for example, will experience God largely through the faculties of their emotions. Experience, emotion, intimacy, and relationship are incredibly important to this group. "Feelers" are more likely to relate to a charismatic expression of the faith, as God can be seen, heard, felt, and known through a relationship with the Holy Spirit.

On the flip side, those who are predominantly "thinkers" will emphasize doctrine and theological precision. Intellectual truths, carefully defined doctrine, liturgy, catechisms, and creeds are incredibly important to this group. "Thinkers" are more likely to relate to the orthodox and reformed expressions of the faith.

But here is where the problem lies: each of us identifies with that which we are most comfortable, which comes most natural, and which accounts for the ways we have most powerfully related to God, *but* we do so to the neglect of the other. So we end up with a sort of theological "stand-off": the "Truthers" vs. "Team Spirit." We either emphasize truth at the expense of emotion, experience, and undervaluing the Spirit, or we emphasize the Spirit, emotion, and experience at the expense of truth. But, God's word calls us to emphasize both!

As Jesus is talking to the "Woman at the Well" in John 4:23, he says, "But the hour is coming, and is now here, when the true worshipers will worship the Father in spirit and truth, for the Father is seeking such people to worship him." Spirit *and* truth! It is both! Who do you think created emotions, senses, and feelings, and gave us the ability to experience the world around us through these faculties? Was it not God? Should we not expect to experience God through them? Are these things in and of themselves originated in sin? No! Of course not! For we see God himself demonstrate these faculties! Conversely, who gave us the Scriptures so that we might know what is true about who God is, how he acts, and the right way for us to follow him? Wasn't this also from God? Thus, it is absolutely essential that we know Jesus intellectually, but it is equally important that we experience him emotionally—as long as the Jesus we're experiencing is consistent with the Jesus of the Bible!

So we see how the way in which we're wired can dramatically affect what we emphasize and what we don't. But there is a second influencer that shapes our biased emphases when approaching Scripture: our story. Where we come from, what we've been through, what has affected us, and what has wounded us, all play a huge role in influencing our perceptions, and consequently, our theology.

Perhaps you come from a church that preached works-based righteousness and have never heard of the free gift of God's never-ending grace offered freely to you by the blood of Jesus. When you do finally hear of this grace (in all its beauty), you might be tempted to swing the pendulum so far in the opposite direction that any mention of "faith producing works" triggers a law-induced allergic reaction. The temptation is to overreact to our previous circumstances in an effort to ensure that we avoid the previous theological error committed by or against us.

But for every action there is an equal and opposite reaction. So, often to the degree we had veered to the left in our previous error, we will overshoot the narrow path and veer an equal degree to the right. We say, "If not works, deeds, obedience, effort, or striving that saves us, then let us flee from these enemies of grace." But if we're not careful, we flee in the opposite direction to an extreme that is just as dangerous. We arrive at a Christianity that promotes a caricature of Biblical grace—one that rejects true discipleship and the call to take up one's cross and follow Jesus.

Perhaps nothing has birthed more heresy in the church and led us to our current situation than the overemphasis of one truth at the expense of another. To so willfully and emphatically elevate one part of a doctrine without giving equal weight to its "opposing" counterpart—to its God-given tension—is an error of grave proportions.

The Bible is full of what could be perceived as contradictions, perhaps none more blatant (or pertinent to the issue at hand) than the apparent conflict between the truths of Ephesians 2:8-9 and James 2:17.

Ephesians 2:8-9 says, "For by grace you have been saved through faith. And this is not your own doing; it is the gift of God, not a result of works, so that no one may boast." But then James 2:17 states, "So also faith by itself, if it does not have works, is dead."

How do we reconcile these two verses and, more importantly, the theologies they represent?

A finite mind will always have a difficult time digesting the truths of an infinite God. What appears to be a contradiction to our finite minds is not a contradiction to God. We think linearly and within space and time, but God is outside space and time; he is transcendent.

Isaiah 55:8 tells us that God's ways and thoughts are higher than ours, so we shouldn't expect to be able to *fully* understand all that God tells us to hold as true. We have to learn to be ok with some things remaining a mystery to us. To do so is actually a posture of worship. It is to understand that God is holy—that he is *other* than us. The Psalmist David understood this: "O LORD, my heart is not lifted up; my eyes are not raised too high; I do not occupy myself with things too great and too marvelous for me" (Psalm 131:1).

Nonetheless, it is our Christian duty to do the difficult labor of seeking to reconcile that which appears to be a contradiction—to hold in tension what could appear to be opposing truths. We can be lazy, however, and we often choose not to do the difficult work of living in the tension in which God has called us to live. So, we cling to the truth that seems the "most" right or "more" right to us, and we let that shape our entire theology. We veer to the left or to the right because the truth we have chosen pulls us in that direction. But in doing so, we have made something equally true the casualty. We have changed the voice of Scripture—the voice of God. We have veered from the narrow path of true discipleship!

We are saved by grace through faith alone, but faith without deeds is dead. If we have Christ we will no longer sin (we will be holy), yet if we do sin (and we will) we have an advocate in Christ. Grace is a free gift, but it demands everything—your whole life. It is free, but costly.

Is it starting to make sense? To preach any one of these things without their counterparts will give us an inaccurate view of the Gospel.

The Gospel message is not complex—giving favor only to those with IQs large enough to digest its complexities. But it *is* hard work to hold the requisite tension of a Biblical understanding of grace and saving faith without placing a biased emphasis in certain places to the neglect of other Biblical truths.

Are you willing to do the hard work?

Throughout Jesus' earthly ministry, he would teach his disciples, often in parables. Rarely was there a teaching session that didn't require Jesus to explain his parables further. Try as they might, his disciples just couldn't seem to understand what exactly he was telling them. Nonetheless, they *tried*. They asked questions, contemplated, and discussed. They *wanted* to understand, so they weren't afraid of putting in the hard work of seeking an understanding of what it was that Jesus was trying to communicate.

We too must be willing to put in the hard work of understanding the tension between grace and the call to follow Jesus with our whole selves—faithfully pursuing obedience and holiness. Being a disciple of Christ demands that we put in the effort.

But take heart, dear Christian. Jesus' disciples never quite "got it" until they received the deposit of the Holy Spirit. Only then did they understand all that Jesus had been doing or saying. Only then were they capable of walking the narrow path. While God is infinite, and his ways are "oh, so much higher" than ours, 1 Corinthians 2:16 tells us that in the Holy Spirit we have the mind of Christ. It is only by intentionally seeking the wisdom, knowledge, and understanding of Christ through the leading of the Holy Spirit that we will be able to walk the narrow path of true discipleship in the divinely orchestrated tension of Biblical faith.

My prayer is that as you continue into the following chapters, you will make the necessary effort to pursue a Spirit-enabled understanding of the mysteries of the Gospel and the tensions held therein, just as I have made every effort to represent them faithfully. In the process, I ask that you will show me grace, seeking to understand what I intend to say (without hearing what I am not saying), and allow every sentence, paragraph, and chapter to be interpreted in light of the book as a whole. This is a very sensitive, yet crucial, topic—one that deserves our full diligence.

III.

GOOD THEOLOGY GONE TOO FAR

The idea that "you didn't save yourself" is what theologians refer to as "Election" (or "Predestination") and is one of the distinguishing doctrines for the theological system known as Calvinism. The key premise of Election is that man in his sin is totally depraved and, left to himself, does not desire God nor does he possess the ability to choose God and believe in him for salvation on his own. He is free to do so, but he won't, for the Scriptures make clear, "None is righteous, no, not one; no one understands; *no one seeks for God.* All have turned aside; together they have become worthless; no one does good, not even one" (Romans 3:10-12, emphasis added). He is free to choose God, but he chooses that which he desires more instead—sin and autonomy.

It follows that, since no man will choose God on his own, God has chosen ("elected") a portion for himself on which to pour out his mercy and grace. Romans 9:10-24 explains:

And not only so, but also when Rebekah had conceived children by one man, our forefather Isaac, though they were not yet born and had done nothing either good or bad—in order that God's purpose of election might continue, not because of works but because of him who calls—she was told, "The older will serve the younger." As it is written, "Jacob I loved, but Esau I hated."

What shall we say then? Is there injustice on God's part? By no means! For he says to Moses, "I will have mercy on whom I have mercy, and I will have compassion on whom I have compassion." So then it depends not on human will or exertion, but on God, who has mercy. For the Scripture says to Pharaoh, "For this very purpose I have raised you up, that I might show my power in you, and that my name might be proclaimed in all the earth." So then he has mercy on whomever he wills, and he hardens whomever he wills.

You will say to me then, "Why does he still find fault? For who can resist his will?" But who are you, O man, to answer back to God? Will what is molded say to its molder, "Why have you made me like this?" Has the potter no right over the clay, to make out of the same lump one vessel for honorable use and another for dishonorable use? What if God, desiring to show his wrath and to make known his power, has endured with much patience vessels of wrath prepared for destruction, in order to make known the riches of his glory for vessels of mercy, which he has prepared beforehand for glory—even us whom he has called, not from the Jews only but also from the Gentiles?

In his grace, God then gives those whom he has elected a new heart, enabling them to respond to the Gospel message in faith. Ezekiel 36:26 reveals, "And I will give you a new heart, and a new spirit I will put within you. And I will remove the heart of stone from your flesh and give you a heart of flesh." Apart from this divine intervention, no one would possess such saving faith. As Jesus contends, "No one can come to me unless the Father who sent me draws him. And I will raise him up on the last day" (John 6:44).

Those whom God saves he also keeps eternally secure. Romans 8:29-30 explains, "For those whom he foreknew he also predestined

to be conformed to the image of his Son.... And those whom he predestined he also called, and those whom he called he also justified,
and those whom he justified he also glorified."

Why is this good news? *Because it means it doesn't depend on us!*

We live in a world driven by performance. If we perform well
enough in high school, we can get into a good college. If we perform
well enough in college, we can graduate with a good enough GPA,
allowing us to get a good job, where if we perform well enough, we
will receive promotions and pay raises.

If that isn't enough, the pressures to perform are starting at an
earlier and earlier age. Competitive preschools require children to
demonstrate cognitive abilities well beyond their age. Youth sports,
music, and theatre have become year-round commitments, unless of
course you want the child to fall below the skill level of his or her
peers.

Even our relationships seem to be increasingly performance
based these days. "Love" seems to be increasingly conditional: "I'm
committed to you until you no longer please me, and then I'm not."

Our culture is obsessed with performance.

But Christian, there is good news: Our salvation, our acceptance
as children of God, and his love for us does not depend on our performance; it depends on Jesus. It's about *his* performance. He did
what we couldn't do. He lived a perfect life and satisfied all the re-
quirements of the law. He then traded us his performance for ours.
He gave us his spoils, and he took our punishment. No longer are we
under the constraints of the law, imprisoned by the demands that we
will inevitably fail to meet; instead we are free. "So if the Son sets you
free, you will be free indeed" (John 8:36).

What's more, *he* changes our hearts, *he* calls us to himself, and *he* sustains us. Grace (and Election) takes the focus off us and puts it where it belongs—on Jesus.

Nonetheless, I have seen the misunderstanding and misuse of this good theology lead to bad inferences and dangerous applications.

I fear there are many of us who are in danger of using (misusing) good theology to justify living an unbiblical Christianity. We have allowed our understanding of grace to excuse us from the responsibility the Bible places on us of choice, decision, and action. We think, *If salvation and sanctification are gifts of grace that are done to us, then we need only to be passive recipients. All obligations to actively participate have been alleviated.*

But if our theology is being used to excuse our own efforts and active participation in seeking to follow and obey Jesus—to earnestly fight sin in our lives and pursue holiness—then I fear our theology is being wielded as a weapon by the Evil One for our destruction.

In 1 Corinthians 4:6, Paul urges the church in Corinth "not to go beyond what is written." And John Calvin echoes this sentiment in his Institutes:

> Human curiosity renders the discussion of predestination, already somewhat difficult of itself, very confusing and even dangerous. No restraints can hold it back from wandering in forbidden bypaths and thrusting upward to the heights. If allowed, it will leave no secret to God that it will not search out and unravel.... Let this, therefore, first of all be before our eyes: to seek any other knowledge of predestination than what the word of God discloses is not less insane than if one should propose to walk in a pathless waste (Job 12:24), or to see in darkness. *And let us not be ashamed to be ignorant of something in this matter* (emphasis added), wherein there is a certain learned ignorance.[7]

We must guard against the temptation to take the ideas put forth by theologians such as Calvin further than the Bible does—even further than Calvin, for that matter. This is where relying on the Holy Spirit to help us hold in tension two seemingly opposing truths becomes absolutely critical, because the moment we allow this otherwise good theology to undermine or negate the burden of personal responsibility that the Scriptures place on us to use our "free will" to respond in faith and obedience, is the moment we have changed the collective voice of the Scriptures. It is the moment we have changed the voice of God and arrived at heresy—holding to a "cheap grace Gospel," which is really no Gospel at all.

Through Faith Alone

We are saved by grace alone. It is what makes the Gospel so scandalous (and even offensive to some). It can't be earned or deserved, only received.

But how do we receive it?

Through faith.

Ephesians 2:8-9 (emphasis added) explains, "For by grace you have been saved *through faith*. And this is not your own doing; it is the gift of God, not a result of works, so that no one may boast."

Grace is the free gift; faith is how we take hold of it. We do this as our lives make evident that we truly believe what we claim to believe—as we respond in action, orientation, and intent to the Gospel of Jesus Christ.

The story of Noah provides a helpful illustration of the marriage between grace and faith—a faith that acts.

Genesis 6:5-8 explains:

The Lord saw that the wickedness of man was great in the earth, and that every intention of the thoughts of his heart was only evil continually. And the Lord regretted that he had made man on the earth, and it grieved him to his heart. So the Lord said, "I will blot out man whom I have created from the face of the land, man and animals and creeping thing and birds of the heavens, for I am sorry that I have made them." But Noah found favor in the eyes of the Lord.

The subsequent verses explain that Noah was righteous and blameless, but does this mean he was without sin? Is this why he had the Lord's favor? Had he earned it? No, I do not believe this to be so. It would be inconsistent with what the Bible teaches about the ramifications of Adam's sin: "Therefore, just as sin came into the world through one man, and death through sin, and so death spread to all men because all sinned" (Romans 5:12). Instead, Genesis 5:9 explains that "Noah walked with God." This can be best understood as: he believed him; he trusted him; and in spite of a proclivity toward sin, he earnestly sought and desired to obey him. Thus, he is credited as righteous and blameless.

Most of us know the story from here. God tells Noah that he is going to flood the earth, but that he will spare him, his wife, his children, and their wives. This is grace. Noah has not earned God's favor. The effects of Adam's sin did not pass him over. He is a sinner just like you and I. But God in his grace decides he is going to spare Noah and his family.

While this is an entirely free, undeserved gift from God, it is contingent upon one thing: Noah must believe God in such a way that it manifests itself in the form of obedience. Noah must build an ark—an endeavor that would undoubtedly take decades to complete. This means in order for Noah to receive God's grace (the sparing of his and his family's lives), he must obey God's command to build the ark.

There is no cheap grace here. The entire trajectory of his life is forever altered. It is grace that God would choose to spare him, but without his response, there is no salvation for Noah or his family. Hebrews 11:7 affirms, "By faith Noah, being warned by God concerning events as yet unseen, in reverent fear constructed an ark for the saving of his household. By this he condemned the world and became an heir of the righteousness that comes by faith."

So it is with us. It is grace that God would send his Son to die for us when we wanted nothing to do with him. It is grace that God would pursue us and offer us forgiveness of sins, the right to become his children, and eternal life. But apart from a substantiated faith, a faith that acts and moves in tangible ways as we reorient our entire lives around following Jesus, there is no salvation. As John 3:36 (emphasis added) makes clear, "Whoever believes in the Son has eternal life; *whoever does not obey the Son shall not see life*, but the wrath of God remains on him."

The origin of faith does not negate the onus of faith

Now some might say, "But the ability to have faith (to believe) is itself God's grace in Election. We only have faith because God enabled us to."

Perhaps this is true, but we must be careful of the inferences we draw from this.

The temptation here is to use God's sovereignty to undermine or negate personal responsibility. If faith is the result of grace, then it is subordinate to it. This would imply that grace justifies apart from faith—making any faith response on our part nonessential to salvation. Instead, we arrive back at a "cheap grace Gospel" where mere belief, disconnected from any subsequent action or surrender, is the mark of a Christian.

While it's not "untrue" that the ability to have faith is the result of God's grace, the inference that it negates personal responsibility *is* (untrue). We must ask, "Is anyone privy to the knowledge of who is elect in advance? Is there any way to know who has received this gift apart from inviting men and women to respond to the Gospel in faith and repentance?" In his series *Thru the Bible*, J. Vernon McGee tells a story of Charles Spurgeon that illustrates this point:

> Someone came to Spurgeon one time and said, "Mr. Spurgeon, if I believed as you do, I would not preach like you do. You say you believe that there are the elect, and yet you preach as if everyone can be saved." Spurgeon's answer was, "They can all be saved. If God had put a yellow streak up and down the backs of the elect, I'd go up and down the streets lifting up shirt tails to find out who had the yellow streak up and down his back. Then I'd give that person the gospel. But God didn't do that. He told me to preach the gospel to every creature and that whosoever will may come." That is our marching order, and as far as I am concerned, until God gives me the roll call of the elect, I am going to preach the "whosoever will" gospel. That is the gospel we are to preach today.[8]

In other words, while we believe that God is busy behind the proverbial curtain on the side of divine sovereignty, we preach that we are responsible to choose to respond to the Gospel (or not). We preach that we must decide to repent of going our own way (sin), choosing to follow Jesus instead. And we preach that it is up to us to start taking seriously what it means to be a disciple of Jesus. We do this because we don't get to see behind the curtain, and as far as we are concerned, Scripture uses the language of choice and decision—accountability and responsibility. Only in hindsight, after we have done all these things in response to the gospel, having completed the race and kept the faith, will we be able to look back and say, "I was chosen in him before the foundation of the world."[9]

Consider Paul, who was able to hold in tension grace and works (Election and free will). In 1 Timothy 1:15 Paul confesses, "The saying is trustworthy and deserving of full acceptance, that Christ Jesus came into the world to save sinners, of whom I am the foremost." Paul understood the gravity of his sin. It was ever before him and it humbled him greatly. Not once did he begin to think he was righteous on his own accord or because of his works. He knew he was saved by grace alone. Nonetheless, he did everything he could to grow in faith and maturity in the Lord. He felt the responsibility that was placed on him to actively participate in his sanctification. Not that in doing so he would be the one sanctifying himself, only that faith carried with it certain implications, and on this side of the proverbial divine curtain, it was his duty (and desire) to run after Christ with his entire being.

This is made quite evident in 1 Corinthians 9:25-27 (NIV):

> Everyone who competes in the games goes into strict training. They do it to get a crown that will not last, but we do it to get a crown that will last forever. Therefore I do not run like someone running aimlessly; I do not fight like a boxer beating the air. No, I strike a blow to my body and make it my slave so that after I have preached to others, I myself will not be disqualified for the prize.

Does Paul believe in Election? Yes. And if anyone had reason to have confidence in his Election it was Paul, who physically encountered Jesus on the road to Damascus and heard an audible call to follow him. And yet, he does not presume upon this Election. Instead, he beats his body, disciplining it in passionate pursuit of the prize (Christ himself). Why? So that he will not be disqualified. So at the end of his life he won't come to find out that he had been mistaken—that he had placed a false confidence in what he understood Election to be. But what's more, it was his joy and delight to follow Jesus, and it was the natural outpouring of a life transformed by grace and lived out in faith. Paul came to count all things as loss compared to the surpassing glory of knowing Christ (Philippians 3:8).

Paul understood Election. He understood theology and right doctrine far better than you or I ever will. And yet he "stayed in his lane." He believed in the sovereignty of God (and he let it influence and encourage him where it should), yet he lived his life practically on the side of human responsibility. And he encouraged us to do the same: "Let us also lay aside every weight, and sin which clings so closely, and let us run with endurance the race that is set before us" (Hebrews 12:1).

Regardless of whether faith originates in God or in man, it is the demonstration of faith in repentance and subsequent discipleship that reveals who is saved. The elect are not those who have intellectually accepted certain doctrinal truths, but those who have exhibited the evidence of faith—those whose lives exhibit fruit that bears witness to a good root. The question is not simply "Do you intellectually believe?" The question is, "Are you born again?" "Do you *walk* by faith?" "Are you *following* Jesus?" "Is your life producing the *fruit* of a disciple?"

This is why Peter urges us:

> For this very reason, make every effort to supplement your faith with virtue, and virtue with knowledge, and knowledge with self-control, and self-control with steadfastness, and steadfastness with godliness, and godliness with brotherly affection, and brotherly affection with love. For if these qualities are yours and are increasing, they keep you from being ineffective or unfruitful in the knowledge of our Lord Jesus Christ. For whoever lacks these qualities is so nearsighted that he is blind, having forgotten that he was cleansed from his former sins. Therefore, *brothers, be all the more diligent to confirm your calling and election,* for if you practice these qualities you will never fall. For in this way there will be richly provided for you an entrance into the eternal kingdom of our Lord and Savior Jesus Christ (2 Peter 1:5-11, emphasis added).

We have called people to "believe" but scarce have preached the holistic, all-encompassing endeavor of discipleship. We have enabled men to feel secure in their "belief" when their lives don't make evident that they have been transformed. Make no mistake: actions/deeds will never make someone elect, but the elect will always exhibit actions/deeds keeping with conversion—not perfectly but pervasively.

The language of Scripture puts the obligation on *us* to repent and believe. It puts the obligation on us to put our faith into action and follow Jesus. And it puts the obligation on us to be active participants in our sanctification. What is happening on God's side of the curtain regarding his sovereign orchestration of things is not for us to fully know or understand.

Faith is about surrender, not performance

How then does this not lead us right back to where we started, relying upon our performance for our justification? How does this not result in a works-based righteousness, as we toil to make certain that we are perfectly obedient, afraid that one act of disobedience might reveal our faith to be insufficient?

The answer is that *the measure of our faith is not in the quality of our performance, but the quantity of our surrender.*

I recently watched an episode of the 1990s television classic, *Boy Meets World*. In the episode, Mr. Feeney is handing back graded exams to his sixth-grade class. He hands back one student's (Rick's) exam and tells him, "Very good work." Next, he gives Corey (the show's main character) back his exam. This time his words are less encouraging. "Not one of your better efforts," he chides, as he places the exam on Corey's desk.

Naturally, Corey peeks over to see what grade Rick received that earned him such praise from Mr. Feeney. When he discovers their grades on the exam are *exactly* the same, he is bewildered. Corey exclaims, "Hey! This isn't fair! Rick and I both got C's. How come you tell him he did good work, and you tell me it wasn't one of my better efforts?"

Mr. Feeney calls Corey to his desk to talk privately where he explains, "Mr. Lewis worked very hard to get his C, and I respect him for that. You, on the other hand, waste your efforts on being class clown."[10]

Corey was apathetic about school, giving half-hearted efforts and spending his time and energy on things he deemed more important.

Rick, on the other hand, was mentally and emotionally present. His heart and devotion were in his class work.

Faith is like that. It's not about our performance or our grade; it's about our commitment. Are we all in, or are we wasting our efforts?

Everyone who hears the Gospel has come from a different place with varying sins, experiences, and sufferings. As a result, everyone is starting their sanctification from a different deficit. Wholehearted devotion might look different for a converted drug dealer or rapist than it does for the convert raised in a Christian home, but grace means that nobody is excluded based on where they've been in the past, or where they are starting as a new Christian. It's ok to be a C student. It's ok to be a D student—so long as you're "all in."

Legalism says you have to be an A student to be saved, while "cheap grace" says all you have to do is show up for class and make a half-hearted effort. A proper understanding of faith debunks both, however. The measure of our faith is not the quality of our performance, but the quantity of our surrender, and Jesus asks us to surrender all. We can (and will) be imperfect, and that's okay, but there is no such thing as being a half-hearted disciple of Jesus.

Totally Depraved No More

There is one final matter we must discuss regarding this topic.

Many of us rightfully believe in the concept of total depravity. This concept correctly ascertains that every part of our being has been infected and affected by sin. This is not to say that we are completely and totally evil, or that we are as evil as we could be, but rather that every part of us is tainted by the effects of sin. Every part of us is, to some degree, corrupted or marred. And while this is true, it is most true regarding the unregenerate man—the non-Christian.

To believe that once we are saved we can still do nothing to change our sinful behavior, however, is to drastically misunderstand what is meant in salvation, in that we have received a new heart, a new nature, and God's Spirit within us. We *were* totally depraved, but we are no longer. We will still wrestle with sin, and life will still uncover remnants of our sinful nature in all parts of our being (and there is grace for that!) *but the chains are broken*. The old nature is put to death. We *are* a new creation, with a new nature, a new heart, and the Spirit of God to help us walk in a new way. This means we *do* have the power (not in and of ourselves, but we have it nonetheless) to change our behavior, to choose to pursue righteousness, and to choose to walk away from any sinful behaviors that we are willfully engaged in.

Many of us are still stuck in a victim mentality regarding our sinful nature. We are still living as if we are slaves to it, waiting idly for God to zap us with his sanctifying power before we attempt to walk in faith and obedience. As a result, we are stuck in the same repetitive cycle of spiritual apathy and immaturity. My hope is that this chapter will begin to deconstruct that dangerous misapplication of otherwise good theology.

* * * * *

I have heard many people decry the words of the classic hymn "I have decided to follow Jesus" on the basis that it represents "decision theology" (the emphasis on man's decision instead of God's sovereignty). While I understand the sentiment that is being protected in doing so, I can't help but lament the sentiment that is lost at the same time.

I fear many of us are stuck in a sort of "spiritual purgatory" because our hearts and minds have been opened to accept the truths of the Gospel—we have "believed"—but we have not made the willful decision to surrender all and follow Jesus.

There is extreme danger in placing too much emphasis on either human responsibility *or* God's sovereignty; we must fight to hold both. We must never lose sight of God's sovereignty—that it is he who saves, that it is he who is the author and perfecter of our faith. But equally as important, we must never lose sight of our responsibility to respond in faith to the invitation of the Gospel—to run after Christ, to discipline ourselves, to throw off all that hinders, to test our faith, and to take up our cross to follow Jesus in life-altering discipleship. Jesus gets the credit, but the responsibility over our choices and actions remains on us.

Christian, have you decided to follow Jesus? The Bible calls you to, and it just might change your life.

> *I have decided to follow Jesus;*
> *The world behind me, the cross before me;*
> *Though none go with me, still I will follow;*
> *My cross I'll carry, till I see Jesus;*
> *Will you decide now to follow Jesus?*
> *No turning back, no turning back.*
>
> *- Sadhu Sundar Singh*

CHAPTER 3 NOTES

[7] John Calvin, *Calvin: Institutes of the Christian Religion*, vol two, ed. J. T. McNeill, (John Knox, Louisville, 2006), eBook ver. 22866-22889. Used by permission.

[8] Taken from *Thru the Bible vol 47: Ephesians* by J. Vernon McGee, p. 31. Copyright © 1991 by J. Vernon McGee. Used by permission of Thomas Nelson. www.thomasnelson.com.

[9] See Ephesians 1:4.

[10] *Boy Meets World,* "Boys II Mensa," directed by David Trainer, written by Michael Jacobs and April Kelly, ABC Studios, October 29, 1993.

PART II:
THE CRISIS OF FAITH

Faith is a belief in a truth that manifests itself in action. It is not mere belief or an intellectual assent to believing that Jesus is who he says he is. It does not exist for a time in the ethereal realm before it requires that you take the proverbial leap. Faith is what happens *when* you leap. It is the point at which belief and action intersect to create forward momentum in a direction that reflects the supposed belief.

The crisis of faith is the moment of contemplation and consideration immediately preceding this action when the cost of the action is weighed against the benefit. Is it worth it? Do I believe that what is to be gained outweighs what it will cost?

As we stand on the precipice of the most important decision we will ever make, it is essential that we realize the full scope of not only what is gained in Christ, but also what it will require that we leave behind.

*"WE POURED FORTH THE UNENDING STREAMS OF GRACE.
BUT THE CALL TO FOLLOW JESUS IN THE NARROW WAY
WAS HARDLY EVER HEARD."*
                                    —DIETRICH BONHOEFFER

IV.

Counting the Cost (Part I)

There is a great cost to becoming a Christian; Jesus makes this clear in Luke 14:26-33. And yet, I fear this is a concept that is foreign to many who claim to have faith in Jesus. After all, we have been taught that the good news of the Gospel is that grace has been offered to us free of charge, free of performance, and free of our own efforts. Assuredly, we didn't just come to this conclusion on our own; it is in fact thoroughly Biblical. Romans 6:23 makes clear, "For the wages of sin is death, but the free gift of God is eternal life in Christ Jesus our Lord." Likewise, Ephesians 2:8-9 (emphasis added) confirms, "For by grace you have been saved through faith. And this is not your own doing; *it is the gift of God*, not a result of works, so that no one may boast." Romans 3:20 adds, "For by works of the law no human being will be justified in his sight."

Jesus paid the price for our salvation with his blood by hanging on a cross and enduring the wrath and forsakenness we deserved.

John 19:30 explains, "When Jesus had received the sour wine, he said, 'It is finished,' and he bowed his head and gave up his spirit." The word for "It is finished" in ancient Greek is *tetelestai*. In Jesus' day, this word was commonly written or stamped on transaction receipts as a way of communicating that the debt owed had been paid in full. As Jesus utters these words with his last breath, he is definitively proclaiming that the debt for our sins has been paid in full.

Salvation cannot be bought with money, nor can it be earned by obedience to the law. What then do I mean by "There is a great cost to becoming a Christian?" More importantly, what does Jesus mean by it?

Shortly after moving to Huntington Beach, California, my wife and I found a townhome to rent. It was probably 40 years old, but one of the biggest draws for me was that it had new windows, new carpet, new countertops, and fresh paint throughout. I don't mind being in a place that's old, but updated features like this can go a long way in making a place seem much newer than it really is.

Much to our surprise, no more than a few weeks after moving in, the paint on the newly painted doors and cabinets began to chip. After a short bit of investigating, we learned the reason the chipping was occurring was because the painters who had been hired to do the job had neglected to scrape off (or at least sand down) the old layer of paint before applying the new one. Since it was oil-based paint, this prevented the new coat from adhering to wood. Instead, the new layer simply dried on top of the old layer, which prevented it from deeply adhering to anything. Unsurprisingly, at the slightest bit of wear and tear, the paint would simply chip off.

Just as you can't put on a new layer of paint without first removing the old layer, the same is true of us spiritually.

We have preached a Gospel that freely extends grace—the forgiveness of sins—without preaching that this free gift is immeasurably costly. We have asked our congregants if they want eternal life and the blessings of God, but we have failed to tell them what this will require of them. "Nothing! It will require nothing of you because Jesus already did everything! Just believe and accept this free offering! Grace! Grace! Grace!" we exclaim. "Just trust that Jesus died for you and put on the new self. Put on Christ, and you will be credited with his righteousness. Your sins will be covered. They will not be held against you. Just believe this and you will be saved!"

While this contains large amounts of incredible and irrefutable truths, it fails to fully account for the Biblical narrative on salvation. For although you have nothing to offer God that would warrant that he show you grace, pardon your sin, adopt you into his family, and give you new/eternal life, God still asks for that which you do have: your life.

In John 3:3, Jesus tells Nicodemus, "Unless one is born again he cannot see the kingdom of God." Romans 6:3-5 explains that this (being born again) occurs by being united with Christ in his death—our old self being crucified with him—and being raised to new life with him in his resurrection.

Ephesians 4:21-24 adds, "Assuming that you have heard about him and were taught in him, as the truth is in Jesus, to put off your old self, which belongs to your former manner of life and is corrupt through deceitful desires, and to be renewed in the spirit of your minds, and to put on the new self, created after the likeness of God in true righteousness and holiness."

So then, to put on the new self first requires that we put off the old self—that we put it to death through repentance and surrender. We must understand the totality of this death of the old self. It is not simply referring to sin as we think of sin. We are called to repent of the entire trajectory of our lives, what we have oriented it around, and the fact that we have gone astray, trying to be our own god. This means we put to death our desires, dreams, ambition, and autonomy.

With it, our claim on our relationships (this includes anger, resentment, and unforgiveness toward others that we might be holding on to); money; possessions; time—even our very life—must also die. In sum, to put to death the old self is to completely and entirely renounce our claim on our own life.

I understand this is quite a departure from "American Christianity," which often highly values chasing our dreams and ambitions. Could Jesus work through our dreams and ambitions? Could he have placed a passion or desire on our hearts because he intends us to pursue it? Absolutely. But not every dream or desire is from the Lord. The unredeemed heart is deceitful above all else, and we will always be fighting against the sinful and selfish temptations of the flesh. We cannot know what is from God and what is simply selfish ambition and self-will for our lives until we have put it all to death, along with our old self. He will resurrect that which is from him.

Friend, have you surrendered so completely? Are you willing to give God your dreams, your future—your life?

Now had Jesus meant the words "believe" and "faith" the way we have come to define them in our modern context—as a mere intellectual assent that is disconnected from an action response—then it would be quite possible to receive salvation apart from the type of cost I have just described. But this is not the case. John 12:37-43 (emphasis added) reads:

> Though he had done so many signs before them, they still did not believe in him, so that the word spoken by the prophet Isaiah might be fulfilled:
>
>> "Lord, who has believed what he heard from us,
>> and to whom has the arm of the Lord been revealed?"
>
> Therefore they could not believe. For again Isaiah said,
>
>> "He has blinded their eyes
>> and hardened their heart,

> lest they see with their eyes,
> > and understand with their heart, and turn,
> > and I would heal them."

...Nevertheless, many even of the authorities believed in him, but for fear of the Pharisees they did not confess it, so that they would not be put out of the synagogue; for they loved the glory that comes from man more than the glory that comes from God.

Here we see that apart from God intervening and removing the veil from our eyes and softening our hearts, we cannot believe. But what about those who *did* receive the grace to believe, but loved the glory that comes from man more than the glory that comes from God? Did their "belief" save them?

No, unfortunately, belief without surrender—without the death of the old self—is an incomplete conversion.

Do not misunderstand; our sin is woven deeper into us than we can possibly imagine. It will be a lifetime process of God unearthing and convicting us of new layers of our depravity, revealing new idols and new sin struggles (and this will be done in the context of a loving relationship). To put the old self to death—to repent of our rebellion—, however, is to resolve in our hearts and minds that what we have and who we are, no longer belongs to us. Whatever God asks for, we will give. Whatever sin he reveals to us, we will surrender. If we willfully decide that we want Christ but are not yet willing to give him control of our lives, then we have not yet put "the old self" to death. Consequently, we are not yet a new creation in Christ.

This was the story of the "rich young ruler" in Matthew 19:16-22:

And behold, a man came up to him, saying, "Teacher, what good deed must I do to have eternal life?" And he said to him, "Why do you ask me about what is good? There is only one who is good. If you would enter life, keep the commandments." He said to him, "Which ones?" And Jesus said, "You shall not murder, You shall not commit adultery, You shall not steal, You shall not bear false witness, Honor your father and mother, and, You shall love your neighbor as yourself." The young man said to him, "All these I have kept. What do I still lack?" Jesus said to him, "If you would be perfect, go, sell what you possess and give to the poor, and you will have treasure in heaven; and come, follow me." When the young man heard this he went away sorrowful, for he had great possessions.

This man came to Jesus, seeking to be affirmed and justified by his works. He asked Jesus which works he must complete to earn salvation, and Jesus responded this would require perfect adherence to the law. Despite Jesus prefacing his statement with a reminder that only one person (Jesus himself) has been perfectly obedient, the "rich young ruler" still contends that he has kept all the commandments. But this is not so, for Jesus knew the ruler's heart had been corrupted by his great wealth. So as the ruler asks what he still lacks, Jesus uses this as an opportunity to point out the man's sin, while offering him an invitation to eternal life in spite of his sin—in spite of his failure to perfectly keep God's laws. He shows him that his wealth has become a stumbling block to him—that he has "played the whore" by prostituting his heart to other gods. But he says, "If you want to be perfect, go, sell what you possess and give to the poor…and come, follow me" (v. 21).

The "rich young ruler" is not perfect—not by any stretch of the imagination; only Jesus is perfect. But the invitation of the Gospel is that we will be counted as righteous (as perfect) if we surrender the claim on our lives and follow after Jesus.

The man in this passage desired eternal life. He desired the kingdom of heaven that Jesus was talking about, but he wanted it in addition to the life he had built, not in place of it. When we preach "cheap grace," we communicate that Christ is an add-on to our current life. We proclaim that we can say, "Jesus, I want what you are offering, but I am not ready to give up *this* part of my life" and still be saved. But the message we see here is one of addition by subtraction. Only if the "rich young ruler" is willing to give up his life is he able to be saved. But he was not ready to give up his claim on his possessions or his wealth—to leave his current life behind and follow after Jesus; thus, he walked away sorrowful—unjustified, unchanged, and unsaved.

Notice that Jesus does not run after him. He does not change his terms. He does not assure or affirm the man it is okay because of grace. He simply lets him walk away to further ponder the cost of the invitation of grace and salvation.

We *must* understand the gravity of this truth: *without surrender and repentance, there is no salvation or conversion, regardless of how clearly we see Jesus to be who he says he is, and regardless of how much we "believe" it!*

We have disconnected faith from discipleship in a way the Bible simply doesn't allow. We have made it "discipleship on our terms," believing we can follow Jesus while maintaining control over our lives, still traveling in the way of our own choosing.

Instead, Jesus defines for us what genuine faith looks like: "If anyone would come after me, let him deny himself and take up his cross and follow me. For whoever would save his life will lose it, but whoever loses his life for my sake will find it" (Matthew 16:24-25). The invitation to follow Jesus is pure, unadulterated grace, but it is just that—an invitation to *follow* him. It is not mere belief, or simply admitting we are weak, inadequate sinners in need of a Savior. There is a necessary response, and that response is giving him everything. In order to gain life, we must lose our lives for Jesus' sake.

Christian, perhaps you heard the message of the Gospel and believed it to be true. Perhaps you desired eternal life and all that Jesus has offered us by grace. Maybe you have started attending church, reading your Bible, and identifying as a Christian—all of which are wonderful things—but have you surrendered control of your life to Jesus?

Jesus is incredibly inclusive. He will let you "date" him; he is approachable. He will engage you, letting you "feel him out" and learn more about him. He is warm and welcoming—to the tax collectors, the prostitutes, and sinners just like you and me. Undoubtedly, he has even gone so far as to pursue us. His offer of salvation does not discriminate regardless of age, gender, race, ethnicity, or our sin-stained past. Nevertheless, while Jesus is inclusive in this manner, conversion is exclusive: it is only for those who have responded to his invitation of grace with repentance, surrender, and discipleship.[11]

I do not say all this to sow unnecessary seeds of worry or doubt about your salvation into your life, nor am I putting any obstacle between you and grace other than that which Jesus himself has made clear. I am not creating a list of legalisms you must adhere to in order to be saved. I am talking about your heart and whether you have surrendered it to Jesus, whether you have let go and given him complete control, and whether you have repented of your old way so that you might walk in a new way.

Christian, it is worth examining whether you have been truly "born again" or are just "dating" Jesus. Are you merely interacting with Jesus in your belief while maintaining control, or are you all in— fully committed and surrendered?

There is a great cost to following Jesus, and we mustn't preach the message of grace without preaching the cost. When we do, we end up with a church full of people who have attempted to put on the "new self" without first putting to death the "old self." But like the paint on the doors and cupboards of our townhouse, the "new self" will not adhere, it will not take root, without first removing the old. Without repentance, surrender, and taking up our cross to follow after Jesus on the narrow path to life, the "new self" will chip off. It will be like the flower that sprouts up quickly on a gravel path, but because it has no roots, when the scorching sun comes, it withers and dies (Matthew 13:5-6).

There is a great cost to taking hold of the free gift of God's grace—the gracious invitation to follow Jesus. But if Jesus is who he says he is, and we really believe this, no cost will be too great.

> *After this many of his disciples turned back*
> *and no longer walked with him. So Jesus said to the twelve, "Do you*
> *want to go away as well?" Simon Peter answered him, "Lord, to whom*
> *shall we go? You have the words of eternal life, and we have believed,*
> *and have come to know, that you are the Holy One of God."*
>
> *-John 6:66-69*

CHAPTER 4 NOTES

[11] *This does not mean our response originates with us. As we talked about in the last chapter, God is sovereignly at work behind the "divine curtain." Those who have surrendered have no reason to boast. Nonetheless, such surrender is our responsibility as far as we can know and understand.*

V.

COUNTING THE COST (PART II): RESPECTABLE IDOLS

There is a great proclivity in the human heart to create and worship idols. This is none more evidenced than in Exodus 32.

God has rescued his people from the bondage of slavery in Egypt and brought them to the foot of Mount Sinai. He has called Moses to ascend the mountain to be in his presence and receive the law written on stone tablets. But as Moses is gone for many days, the people grow restless and ask Aaron to make them gods so they may worship them. Aaron collects pieces of gold jewelry from the people, melts them down, and out of this forms a golden calf. The people take the calf and present it before the assembly and proclaim, "These are your gods, O Israel, who brought you up out of the land of Egypt!" (Exodus 32:4)

Representing both great irony and great tragedy, it is as God is writing the law, calling for total allegiance—commanding that his people have no other gods before him but love him with their whole heart, mind, and soul—that the people below are creating false gods to worship.

The Israelites had witnessed, even experienced, God faithfully rescuing them from captivity in mighty and miraculous ways, and yet here they were, offering their praise to that which they fashioned with their own hands! Isaiah 44:14-17 highlights the irrationality of such an action:

> He cuts down cedars, or he chooses a cypress tree or an oak and lets it grow strong among the trees of the forest. He plants a cedar and the rain nourishes it. Then it becomes fuel for a man. He takes a part of it and warms himself; he kindles a fire and bakes bread. Also he makes a god and worships it; he makes it an idol and falls down before it. Half of it he burns in the fire. Over the half he eats meat; he roasts it and is satisfied. Also he warms himself and says, "Aha, I am warm, I have seen the fire!" And the rest of it he makes into a god, his idol, and falls down to it and worships it. He prays to it and says, "Deliver me, for you are my god!"

While the absurdity of the Israelites' actions might seem obvious to us, idolatry is not limited to a "stiff-necked and hard-hearted" people of the ancient Near East; it is a by-product of the fall and common to *all* mankind.

The sinful man rejects God, not wanting to submit to his covering—not wanting to be accountable for his sin—yet recognizes a "God void" that must be filled. He was created to worship, after all. So he finds someone or something else to put in the place of God and toward which to direct his love, devotion, and praise.

Romans 1:19-25 sheds further light on this proclivity:

> For what can be known about God is plain to them, because God has shown it to them. For his invisible attributes, namely, his eternal power and divine nature, have been clearly perceived, ever since the creation of the world, in the things that have been made. So they are without excuse. For although they knew God, they did not honor

him as God or give thanks to him, but they became futile in their thinking, and their foolish hearts were darkened. Claiming to be wise, they became fools, and exchanged the glory of the immortal God for images resembling mortal man and birds and animals and creeping things.

Therefore God gave them up in the lusts of their hearts to impurity, to the dishonoring of their bodies among themselves, because they exchanged the truth about God for a lie and worshiped and served the creature rather than the Creator, who is blessed forever! Amen.

I must confess, I do not know anyone (although I am sure many still exist) who carves an image out of wood or precious metals, builds a shrine around it, calls it his or her god, and offers worship and sacrifice to it. But this is what makes idolatry so dangerous to the Christian today. Rarely does it exist in such an overt fashion anymore.

Idols are not limited to that which is made by human hands, nor is idolatry restricted to that which is innately sinful; rather, it is a sin of the heart. It occurs when we ascribe to anything (good or bad) the love, devotion, or praise that belongs to God alone. It is when we put our greatest hope in something other than Jesus and his Gospel.

Jerry Bridges has written a book titled *Respectable Sins*. In this book, Bridges brings light to the fact that a whole host of sins exist in our lives that are pervasive, yet go largely unchecked because they are considered less taboo within the modern Christian culture. Sins like adultery, stealing, drunkenness, and coarse language, for example, might be frowned upon, but sins like autonomy, selfish ambition, and gluttony do not carry the same stigma. These sins, which have become commonplace in the church, are tolerated, accepted, and sometimes even celebrated. They, for lack of a better word, have become "respectable."

The same is true with idolatry. A "respectable idol" occurs when what is innately (and often exceedingly) good, begins to steal our affections for Jesus. Instead of pointing us and our worship toward

God as the creator and giver of all good gifts, our affections are directed toward the gifts themselves. Like respectable sins, respectable idols go largely unchecked and at times are even justified or affirmed by the Christian culture as a whole.

As we talk about counting the cost of following Jesus, we might readily accept that we must lay down the idols in our lives that are innately sinful, or the idols that are sometimes more taboo, like work, material gain, or concern over our physical appearance, but what about the more "respectable" idols? Do we understand that we must surrender these to follow Jesus as well?

As we talk about respectable idols, there is perhaps not a more challenging passage in all of Scripture than Luke 14:25-33. Only here do we really get an accurate sense of the magnitude of Jesus' insistence that we count the cost before becoming his disciple—and of the subtlety, pervasiveness, and deception of the idols to which we cling the tightest.

Luke 14:25-33 reads:

Now great crowds accompanied him, and he turned and said to them, "If anyone comes to me and does not hate his own father and mother and wife and children and brothers and sisters, yes, and even his own life, he cannot be my disciple. Whoever does not bear his own cross and come after me cannot be my disciple. For which of you, desiring to build a tower, does not first sit down and count the cost, whether he has enough to complete it? Otherwise, when he has laid a foundation and is not able to finish, all who see it begin to mock him, saying, 'This man began to build and was not able to finish.' Or what king, going out to encounter another king in war, will not sit down first and deliberate whether he is able with ten thousand to meet him who comes against him with twenty thousand? And if not, while the other is yet a great way off, he sends a delegation and asks for terms of peace. So therefore, any one of you who does not renounce all that he has cannot be my disciple."

Make no mistake: the Bible's emphasis for us to love one another is pervasive. What's more, we have been commanded to care for our families. We are told that neglecting to do so makes us "worse than an unbeliever" (1 Timothy 5:8). In Ephesians 5:25, we are told that husbands are to love their wives as Christ loves the church, even giving himself up for her. So what does Jesus mean that we are to hate our fathers and mothers, wives and children, brothers and sisters?

The use of the word "hate" in this instance does not adhere to the traditional definition. Jesus is not suggesting we harbor disdain for these people; rather, the word is used as a metric of comparison. It is a word chosen to show the supreme allegiance to Christ in our lives above all else. As far as the heavens are above the earth, so should our love and loyalty to Christ be above that of any other allegiance we might have.

There is often no conflict between the love and loyalty we have for our families and our commitment in discipleship to following Jesus. The Bible makes it clear that following Jesus means sacrificially giving yourself to these relationships. There are times, however, familial obligations/allegiances and following Jesus *are* in opposition to one another. When this is the case, we must be willing to lay even these relationships down to follow Jesus.

An Example from Marriage

A few years back, an article about marriage made its way around the social media sites titled "Marriage is Not for You." In the well-intended article, the newlywed author recounts a conversation where his father bestowed upon him the wisdom that marriage was about his spouse and not about him. While I fully agree with the overall sentiment of the article (that marriage requires us to die to ourselves and our selfish desires), I think as Christians we miss something if we stop there.

The article seemed to suggest the primary purpose of marriage is to love our spouses selflessly. I have heard many Christian couples echo this sentiment as well. They express how marriage has revealed just how selfish they are, and that God's primary purpose for marriage is to sanctify them by teaching them how to love selflessly as Christ does. While this is undoubtedly a characteristic of marriage, I do not believe it is God's primary purpose for marriage.

Biblically, the first example of a marriage is in the Garden of Eden. God has just finished creating the world and everything in it. He placed Adam in the Garden and appointed him to name all the living creatures, while helping care for and cultivate the garden (Genesis 2:15). *After* God has assigned Adam this purpose, he reaches this profound conclusion: "It is not good that man should be alone. I will make him a helper fit for him" (v. 18).

The term *helper* does not mean the woman has any less value or worth than the man. Genesis is clear that both man and woman are equal image bearers and therefore of equal value and worth. It does mean, however, that God did not create Eve for Adam so that Eve would become his new purpose, but so that Eve could help Adam with the purpose God had already assigned him.

When we try to define the purpose of marriage as "loving our spouses selflessly," the marriage becomes its own end; it takes on an inward focus. Martin Luther once said, "Sin is the self caving in on itself" (author's paraphrase). In other words, it is the self trying to meet its own perceived needs.

Now, in the case of marriage, the man and woman have become one. For the sake of this explanation, we will name this new person formed from the original two, "Matrimony." If Matrimony now makes its primary focus to meet the needs of Matrimony (husband meeting the needs of wife or vice versa), are not they still making the same sinful error that Martin Luther speaks of in his quote? Is that not still the self trying to meet its own perceived needs—the self caving in on itself? What seems to be selfless in putting our spouses first is actually still self-serving regarding God's greater purpose for marriage.

This is actually the very reason Paul says it is better NOT to marry (1 Corinthians 7:32-35). He says the husband will be so busy trying to please the wife and the wife will be so busy trying to please the husband that they will be distracted from their devotion to the Lord. In other words, instead of being more productive as a team for the kingdom, they will actually render themselves less effective by being consumed with meeting each other's needs. In 1 Corinthians 7:35 (NIV) Paul explains, "I am saying this for your own good, not to restrict you, but that you may live in a right way in undivided devotion to the Lord."

Marriage itself is not the problem; the problem is when marriage becomes an end unto itself. We have been charged with the command to seek first the kingdom of heaven (Matthew 6:33), and God's original design for marriage was that it would be a means to that end. But marriage and family have become a form of "justified idolatry" in Western Christianity. We are using marriage and children as an excuse to be inwardly focused—to abandon the call to "seek first the Kingdom of Heaven" because, after all, we are told "family is your first ministry." We are getting married, turning inward, becoming consumed with building our own households, chasing our own dreams (or the dreams of our spouses and children), and seeking our own kingdoms first.

Jesus laid down his life for the church (and we as husbands should lay down ours for our wives), but he didn't stop there. He didn't love her (the church) by simply seeking to make her temporally happy (although sometimes loving her includes this). Laying down his life for her was not an end unto itself, but rather a means to a greater end: he called her to follow after him, to die to her own vision for her life, and to join a greater mission. In the same way, we have to lead our marriages (and families) toward something greater than the marriage and the family unit. We have to love our families toward a greater end than merely each other.

Jesus as the "End"

At the point of conversion, we are willfully resolving to surrender all to follow Jesus—to seek first the kingdom of heaven above all else. We are surrendering all our attachments, our control over the things we love most, and our idols.

An "idol" is anything that stands in the way of the call to seek Christ and his kingdom above all else. An "idol" is that for which we say, "I love you, Jesus, but...." It is that for which we are willing to compromise, disobey, sin, or neglect the call of God. We might say, "I love you, Jesus, and I desire to take up my cross and follow you, but if I don't compromise or sin here and in this way, I might lose this person or thing that I love."

There are no caveats to the call that Jesus makes to follow him in discipleship. As we saw with the "rich young ruler," the call to follow Jesus means we surrender in our hearts all that is most dear to us, even that which seems the most innocuous to us. We might justify certain forms of idolatry and attachment, but Jesus makes clear, "Any one of you who does not renounce all that he has cannot be my disciple" (Luke 14:33).

We are most satisfied in Jesus when he is our end. But when we cling to idols we make Jesus the means to a greater end—an end that can't satisfy—that can't lead to life, but only to death.

In the fictional story *The Great Divorce*, C.S. Lewis brilliantly illustrates how idolatry hinders us from experiencing God and the blessings therein. The story imagines a bus that travels back and forth between hell and heaven. Anyone in hell is free to get on the bus and travel to heaven, and in turn, to take the bus back to hell if they so choose.

One particular woman, Pam, arrives in heaven in hopes of being reunited with her son, Michael. You see, in life, Michael had been this woman's greatest love; he had given her purpose and value. As she arrives in heaven, it is not in hopes of seeing or knowing Jesus. But, she certainly is open to Jesus if Jesus means that seeing her son will be expedited (as her conversation with a heavenly spirit illustrates):

"I'll do whatever's necessary. What do you want me to do? Come on. The sooner I begin it, the sooner they'll let me see my boy. I'm quite ready."

"But, Pam, do think! Don't you see you are not beginning at all as long as you are in that state of mind? You're treating God only as a means to Michael. But the whole (process) consists in learning to want God for His own sake."[12]

The attachment for her son is so great that she has no interest in getting to know God for his own sake. She has no patience for a long, drawn-out process. The more she is kept from her son, the more irate she becomes:

"Give me my boy. Do you hear? I don't care about all your rules and regulations. I don't believe in a God who keeps mother and son apart. I believe in a God of love. No one had a right to come between me and my son. Not even God. Tell Him that to His face. I want my boy, and I mean to have him. He is mine, do you understand? Mine, mine, mine, for ever and ever."[13]

This woman becomes so indignant that she willfully gets on the bus to return to hell.

When we love anything more than God, even if that thing is a good thing he has given us and commanded us to love, it begins to subtly turn our hearts against God. We cling to this thing and we let it orchestrate our steps. We let it dictate the direction of our lives. We turn from the narrow path. If the Lord were to take this thing from us, it would elicit anger, doubt, and even hatred toward God, for God himself was never enough to us. He was but a means to the greater end of that which we truly desired.

So the question is, have you truly counted the radical cost of following Jesus? What are the "respectable idols" to which you are still clinging?

Renouncing these things does not mean we eradicate them from our lives. Rather, it means we pry open the close-fisted grip our hearts have on them and prayerfully surrender control of them to the Lord. It means we give him permission to do what he deems best with these things, and it means we commit wholeheartedly to following Jesus even when it costs us the things (or even the people) we have loved most. We hold everything with an open hand and say, "Even this, God. Even this I give over to you." Then, we ask him to fill the void with a deeper love for him. We ask him to teach us to love him for his own sake.

We tend to think the greatest threats to following Jesus are the sins we consider vile—sins like lust and adultery. But in reality, it is the "respectable idols" that we hold most dear to our hearts that often pose the greatest threat.

In *The Great Divorce*, shortly after the interaction between the mother and the spirit, there is another encounter. This time, there is a man who has a lizard-like beast growing from his shoulder. The beast represents the man's fleshly desire for sensuality. It is this "lust" that has hindered him from surrendering himself to God. After much back-and-forth between this man and an angel, the man surrenders himself and gives the angel permission to remove the beast, no matter how painful it will be.

Having witnessed both these interactions, the story's main character asks incredulously:

"But am I to tell them at home that this man's sensuality proved less of an obstacle than that poor woman's love for her son? For that was, at any rate, an excess of love."

To which his teacher responds:

"Ye'll tell them no such thing," he replied sternly. "Excess of love, did ye say? There was no excess, there was defect. She loved her son too little, not too much. If she had loved him more there'd be no difficulty. I do not know how her affair will end. But it may well be that at this moment she's demanding to have him down with her in hell. That kind is sometimes perfectly ready to plunge the soul they say they love in endless misery if only they can still in some fashion possess it. No, no. Ye must draw another lesson. Ye must ask, if the risen (redeemed) body even of (lust) is as grand...as ye saw, what would the risen body of maternal love or friendship be?"[14]

When we love God above all else, all other loves fall into their rightful place and find their greatest expression. We cannot love others if we don't first love God more than anything else. Instead, our love will be defective and self-serving, wounding us and the one we claim to love.

Love seeks the best interest of that which we claim to love, and the best interest of another is always to lead him toward the source of life (God himself). It doesn't seek merely that person's temporal happiness, but his or her eternal prosperity. Only by surrendering our attachments to take hold of Christ above all else can we truly love anything or anyone else in the way God intended.

Are you beginning to see why Jesus says that few will enter the narrow gate that leads to life (Matthew 7:14)? For many of us, it is not because we are unable to intellectually ascend to the Gospel truths. Rather, it is because the cost is too great. The gift of grace, although free, is too costly to take hold of. Perhaps we could surrender some of our less-enviable qualities and traits. Perhaps we could go to church and read our Bibles more and do our best not to swear or engage in sexual promiscuity. But to surrender our deepest-rooted idols is too much. It is unimaginable that we would pray, "Lord, I give to You all that is dearest to me and entrust it in Your hands. I give You permission to take from me my parents, my spouse, my children, my brothers and sisters, and my friends, if that be Your will. I give You permission to take my dreams, my job, my finances, and my status. I entrust it all to You and renounce my claim on it. I surrender all to You, Lord Jesus."

And yet this is the cost that Jesus asks us to count in Luke 14. This is what it means to take up our cross and follow Jesus along the narrow path. But don't forget, this is also the way to life and life abundant.

Grace is free, and yet it costs you all that you have. Grace is costly, but it gives you immeasurably more.

> "You make known to me the path of life;
> in your presence there is fullness of joy;
> at your right hand are pleasures forevermore."
> –Psalm 16:11

CHAPTER 5 NOTES

12 THE GREAT DIVORCE by C.S. LEWIS copyright © C.S. Lewis Pte. Ltd. 1946. Extracts reprinted by permission. (HarperCollins Publishers, New York, 1973), 98-99.

13 Ibid., 102-103.

14 Ibid., 114-115.

VI.

THE IMMEASURABLY MORE

How can something so costly be good news?

In Matthew 13:44 (NIV), Jesus gives us the answer: "The kingdom of heaven is like treasure hidden in a field. When a man found it, he hid it again, and then in his joy went and sold all he had and bought that field." For this man, affording to buy the field literally costs him everything he has. And yet, he rejoices as he heads home to sell it all because in light of what is to be gained in buying the field, "all he had" is a trivial price to pay.

No matter the cost of following Jesus, it does not compare to what is gained. Although it costs us everything we have, it gives us immeasurably more; it gives us God himself. In this is life.

The Secret to Life

Life is found when we let go of the pursuit of the life we think will make us happy.

If we're honest, we all spend our lives pursuing the things we think will make us happy, satisfy us, and complete us. We spend our lives trying to gratify our desires, chase our dreams, and meet our perceived needs. Yet it seems the more we chase these things, the further away happiness becomes. In Greek philosophy, this was known as the hedonistic paradox. The philosophers realized the more they pursued happiness and pleasure, the more elusive it became. Why is this?

The world tells us to follow our hearts, to do what feels good, and to chase after what we think will make us happy. But the truth is, we don't know what is best for ourselves. There is a huge gap between our perceived needs and our actual needs. Often times our perceived "needs" are simply our "wants." They are what the devil is currently using to tell us the lie that "if we just had this job, or this relationship, or this amount of money, or this family, or this fame, or these social media followers, then we'd be happy." But the moment we attain one of those things, the lie changes. We never quite arrive at happiness or contentment—at least not for more than a week or two. We're always one big life change away from it.

But what if this very pursuit is killing us? Depression, anxiety, despair, and restlessness are at an all-time high (I've battled them myself). What if being the "master of our fate and the captain of our soul" is why we're so miserable? What if we were never intended to have this role? What if the effects of sin are so damaging that it becomes impossible to accurately discern what is best for us?

One pastor put it well: "No one is worse to you than you are." If you think about it, while many people have been the victim of undeniable atrocities, for most people, it is the decisions we have made while chasing a desire, 'following our heart,' or trying to meet a per-ceived need that have caused us the most heartache. It is these deci-sions that have left us empty, broken, anxious, and depressed. Prov-erbs 14:12 explains, 'There is a way that seems right to a man, but its end is the way to death.' Proverbs 8:35-36 adds, 'For whoever finds me [wisdom/righteousness] finds life and obtains favor from the LORD, but he who fails to find me injures himself.'"

Perhaps the most memorable book I read during my childhood was *Where the Red Fern Grows* by Wilson Rawls. The book tells the story of a young boy and his raccoon-hunting dogs. While over time I have forgotten much of the book, one part has stayed with me.

As the young boy is learning the ways of raccoon hunting, his grandfather reveals a "trick" that guarantees success in catching a raccoon. ...simply take a hollowed-out log and drill a small hole in it just large enough for a raccoon to barely fit his hand into it. Next, place a small, metallic, shiny object in the hole. Something as simple as a small piece of aluminum foil will work perfectly. The shiny object will draw the raccoon's attention. Fixating on the object, he will im-mediately try to retrieve it. As the raccoon reaches into the hole and closes his hand around the object, his closed fist will now be too large to come back out through the hole. If the raccoon would just drop the shiny object, he would get away, but he won't do it. He will remain there—trapped—until he starves to death or is killed by the hunter or another animal.[15]

It seems silly to us, doesn't it? And for a worthless piece of alu-minum foil? "DUDE! Just let go of the shiny object! Don't you know it's killing you? Let go! Live!"

But we do the same thing. Jesus says, "If anyone would come af-ter me, let him deny himself and take up his cross and follow me. For whoever would save his life will lose it, but whoever loses his life for my sake will find it" (Matthew 16:24-25). We have failed, however, to grasp the gravity of this passage—to realize what this verse is saying—what it is asking of us. Life is found in Jesus alone, and he says if you're going to come with him, you have to let go of the aluminum foil—the life you think is going to bring you joy, fulfillment, and contentment. Yes, it's shiny and promises to satisfy, but it never will. In fact, it is keeping you from *true* life.

The Lord is beckoning you to follow him, and in doing so to find the life you so badly desire. But you can't follow him if your hand is stuck in the tree stump with your fist tightly grasping onto the vision you have for your life. Being a Christian is about more than mere belief; it is faith put into action. It's trusting in the goodness and love of God with your life.

What would it look like for you to trust God with your whole life—for you to surrender control to him? What would it look like to die to your own desires and become a follower of Jesus? What would it look like to live your life for Jesus instead of for self? What is your "aluminum foil"?

I leave you with the testimony of a young woman who wrestled with these very questions when confronted with Jesus' words in Matthew 16:25 (see previous):

My heart cried out, "Oh, no, not that! I do not want to lose my life. I want to live! I want happiness and beautiful things and friends. I want (joy) and popularity and a good time. I want life!" A sadness which seemed about to crush the breath out of my body engulfed me. How unfair, how cruel, how crazy—to ask me to give up life when it was the one thing I longed for—life with its music, its color, it's fun!

I listened to the sermon. Step by step the way was explained; the logic irrefutable; the paradox seemed unanswerable, so maddeningly convincing, and yet I was unwilling to accept it. It was impossible for me to give up my life whatever the promises. Then the last hymn was announced: "When I survey the wondrous cross." My eyes skimmed down over the verses. Then something like panic seized me. There was a line coming which I could not sing. Nothing could make me sing that—I would die if I had to. The second stanza of the hymn began; the first line, then the second line—it was coming nearer; what should I do? How could I give up everything? It was asking too much. "O God," I cried in my heart, "what shall I do?"

Then moved by some power not of myself, I managed to sing, inaudibly, "All the vain things that charm me most, I sacrifice them to His blood." It was done! Everything was gone. At that moment life seemed drained of everything. It was complete and utter emptiness. There was nothing left. But at that very moment, almost simultaneously, came an overflowing of breathless joy. It seemed that I would be swept off my feet so great was the infilling, the glory. Christ Himself flooded my heart, overwhelmed me with love. In a flash it was plain—this was life, this abundance, this joy unspeakable and full of glory.[16]

Life is found when we let go of the pursuit of the life we think will make us happy—when we make Jesus the Master of our fate and the Captain of our soul. For this job was never meant for us, but for him alone.

CHAPTER 6 NOTES

[15] Wilson Rawls, *Where the Red Fern Grows,* (Laurel-Leaf, New York, 1961), 55-56.

[16] E. Stanley Jones, *Conversion,* (©1959 Abingdon Press. Used by Permission. All rights reserved.), 56.

"*I CAN SAY THAT I NEVER KNEW WHAT JOY WAS LIKE UNTIL I GAVE UP PURSUING HAPPINESS, OR CARED TO LIVE UNTIL I CHOSE TO DIE. FOR THESE TWO DISCOVERIES I AM BEHOLDEN TO JESUS.*"

— MALCOLM MUGGERIDGE

.

PART III:
THE JOURNEY OF
FAITH

There was nothing particularly special about that day; in many ways it was the same as any other. Christopher was out making his deliveries on foot, just as he did every day.

He typically began every morning at the first sign of light. If he hurried, he could deliver all the packages to the people who lived in town before the weather got too hot. In the afternoons, he would travel to make his deliveries to the farmers in the surrounding countryside by using the trail that cut through the forest. The shade of the oak trees that lined the trail was a welcome reprieve from the afternoon sun.

But for some reason, on this particular day, Christopher chose to cut through the forest first before going into town. It was curiosity, mostly. He wanted to see the way the forest looked as the rays of sun burst through the canopies, causing the morning dew to glisten.

With each step he saw the beauty of the forest in a new way. Everything sparkled. It was as if God himself had painted the trees, the grass, the leaves, and the wild flowers, and then covered them all with diamonds.

"That was a funny thought," he laughed to himself. God wasn't something Christopher usually gave much consideration.

This morning, however, was different. He could feel something stirring in him. It was as if the forest was beckoning to him. Usually Christopher tried to finish his delivery route as quickly as he could, but this morning he didn't seem to want it to end. So he walked extra slow, taking in every detail, pausing to admire the beauty. Perhaps this is why he noticed the divergent trail, a trail he had never noticed before, just to the right of the bend ahead.

It was overgrown for certain. It looked as if no one had been on it for quite some time. But it was mesmerizing, in a wild, untamed-beauty sort of way. There were wildflowers with the most vibrant colors he'd ever seen—reds, purples, yellows. There were low-hanging vines that stretched over a little babbling creek. Even the weeds, as they glistened in the morning dew, were breathtaking.

As Christopher got closer, he noticed a small, carefully carved wooden sign, right at the fork. It wasn't hidden, but a low-hanging branch made certain that if you weren't looking for it—if you were moving in haste, caught up in the worries of the day—you would never notice it; Christopher hadn't. The sign read:

This way—Truth and Life. →

Christopher couldn't explain it, but for some reason he believed the sign. For some reason he felt he was supposed to find it. He began to think about the day. Why had he changed his route? Why had he changed his routine? Why today? Was it just a coincidence? Or was this the answer to the emptiness?

Christopher had long struggled with a restlessness he couldn't quite explain—with the thought there must be more to life than the hustle and bustle of the world around him.

There was only one way to find out.

As Christopher started to move toward the path, a strange thought passed across his mind: If I go this way, there is no coming back. Despite the emptiness he had felt in his current life, a sadness came over him as he thought about leaving it behind. It was comfortable. It was safe and predictable; it was all that he knew.

He just stood there for what seemed like hours—contemplating in his mind the decision before him. Do I cling to what I know, and continue on the path I've traveled thousands of times? Or do I leave it all behind and find truth and life? Do I really believe the sign? Do I really believe it is the way to truth and life?

A few more minutes passed. He turned around to look at the way he had come; then he turned back to the path before him—the less-traveled path. "I believe," he said aloud. And with that, he walked into the unknown.

Christopher considered and contemplated the cost of following the path leading to truth and life. He wrestled with the decision and all it would mean for his life moving forward. Convinced that the promise of the sign was true, he turned from the course he was on and forever altered the direction of his life, moving in faith toward a new destination.

But what comes after that?

How we think about this next aspect of the Christian life is of the utmost importance. The call to follow Jesus is a call to divert from the trajectory of our former lives in favor of a new direction. Here, it is helpful (and Biblical) to view Christian discipleship in the image of a journey. This section is about just that: the Christian's holistic embarkation upon the journey of faith.

Perhaps you're nervous about embarking on such an adventure. Perhaps you're wondering, *Where are we going? How do we get there?*

Are we traveling alone? Is it safe? These are all questions we will seek to answer in Part III.

One thing is certain, though: nothing will ever be the same.

VII.

Set Your Heart on Pilgrimage

All of life is ultimately a pursuit. We all wake up each day and seek after *something* as our greatest destination. We all treasure *something* above all else that we yearn for—that our heart and flesh cry out for—and, as a result, our daily actions reflect this as we strive, toil, and put forth effort toward this end.

For the non-believer, this pursuit is ultimately an extension of the Fall. God is rejected in favor of our own wants, desires, and autonomy. But as we lay down *this* pursuit, it doesn't mean we hereby cease any and *all* pursuits. Christian discipleship is not the absence of pursuit. Something will always occupy that slot of what we ultimately value and desire, and this will shape the trajectory of the perpetual forward momentum of our everyday lives.

By putting our faith in Jesus, we are effectively re-orienting the entire trajectory of our lives. We have a new treasure—a new ultimate destination—which we are actively and intentionally pursuing: God himself.

This is essential: we are not merely asking Jesus into our hearts to accompany us as we continue on the way of our own choosing. Don't get me wrong, there is important truth in this sentiment of asking Jesus into our hearts. It represents belief and decision, and Jesus *does* make us his dwelling place through the deposit of the Holy Spirit. Nonetheless, we mustn't miss the reorienting of our path that occurs in salvation. We mustn't relegate discipleship to sinning less and praying more while continuing to orient our lives in pursuit of lesser ends. This is why Jesus so frequently uses the language "follow me" as a Gospel invitation: it highlights the change of direction that must occur. In faith, we are setting our hearts on him above all else.

The Bible (specifically the Old Testament) uses the word "pilgrimage" to describe a journey in pursuit of God and his presence. Psalm 84:1-7 (NIV, emphasis added) reads:

> How lovely is your dwelling place, Lord Almighty! My soul yearns, even faints, for the courts of the Lord; my heart and my flesh cry out for the living God. Even the sparrow has found a home, and the swallow a nest for herself, where she may have her young—a place near your altar, Lord Almighty, my King and my God. Blessed are those who dwell in your house; they are ever praising you. *Blessed are those whose strength is in you, whose hearts are set on pilgrimage.* As they pass through the Valley of Baka, they make it a place of springs; the autumn rains also cover it with pools. They go from strength to strength, till each appears before God in Zion.

In the Old Testament, a pilgrimage was a physical journey to the temple atop Mount Zion. As Israel's story unfolded, God's people were scattered throughout the surrounding lands. Three times a year (for the feasts of Passover, Weeks, and Booths) those who lived outside Jerusalem—far from Mount Zion—would set out on a journey to the temple to make the necessary sacrifices for the atonement of their sin and to visit the presence of the Lord. The journey was often long and arduous, taking the pilgrims through difficult and dangerous terrain. But the longing for the Lord—to be in his presence and experience him more—gave them strength as they made the trip. It was well worth the cost.

The temple represented God's presence amongst Israel. Inside the temple, in the inner courts, there was a room called the Holy of Holies, where God's presence resided. No one but the High Priest, however, was allowed into the inner courts, entering fully into his presence. As Hebrews 9:6-8 explains:

> These preparations having thus been made, the priests go regularly into the first section, performing their ritual duties, but into the second only the high priest goes, and he but once a year, and not without taking blood, which he offers for himself and for the unintentional sins of the people. By this the Holy Spirit indicates that the way into the holy places is not yet opened as long as the first section is still standing.

The temple was never supposed to be a permanent solution. Hebrews tells us it was but a shadow of what was to come. The sacrificial system of shedding the blood of animals to atone for sin was put into place to restrain behavior and point forward to Jesus, but it could not change the heart of a man. It could do nothing about his sinful nature. Hebrews 9:9-10 tells us, "According to this arrangement, gifts and sacrifices are offered that cannot perfect the conscience of the worshiper, but deal only with food and drink and various washings, regulations for the body imposed until the time of reformation."

When Jesus came, he satisfied the demands of the law and the sacrificial system in a much greater way. While the blood of animals, shed on the earthly altar, covered over sin for a time, the blood of Jesus, shed in the heavenly places, put away sin forever. No longer is there a need for the annual sacrifice atoning for sin. No longer is there a veil separating the people from the Holy of Holies and the presence of God.

Hebrews 9:23-26 makes clear:

> It was necessary for the copies of the heavenly things to be purified with these rites, but the heavenly things themselves with better sacrifices than these. For Christ has entered, not into holy places made with hands, which are copies of the true things, but into heaven itself, now to appear in the presence of God on our behalf. Nor was it to offer himself repeatedly, as the high priest enters the holy places every year with blood not his own, for then he would have had to suffer repeatedly since the foundation of the world. But as it is, he has appeared once for all at the end of the ages to put away sin by the sacrifice of himself.

As a result, we now have direct access to the King, his throne, and his presence. Hebrews 10:19-22 expounds:

> Therefore, brothers, since we have confidence to enter the holy places by the blood of Jesus, by the new and living way that he opened for us through the curtain, that is, through his flesh, and since we have a great priest over the house of God, let us draw near with a true heart in full assurance of faith, with our hearts sprinkled clean from an evil conscience and our bodies washed with pure water.

No longer is there need to make the physical journey to Jerusalem—to the temple on Mount Zion—to be near to God. Remember, this was but a shadow of a greater reality. Instead, Jesus has brought us spiritually near to him—into the heavenly Jerusalem:

> But you have come to Mount Zion and to the city of the living God, the heavenly Jerusalem, and to innumerable angels in festal gathering, and to the assembly of the firstborn who are enrolled in heaven, and to God, the judge of all, and to the spirits of the righteous made perfect, and to Jesus, the mediator of a new covenant, and to the sprinkled blood that speaks a better word than the blood of Abel" (Hebrews 12:22-24).

The sacrifice has been made, the debt has been paid, sin has been dealt with, and we have been brought near. Paul tells us we are God's temple now: "Do you not know that you are God's temple and that God's Spirit dwells in you?" (1 Corinthians 3:16)

If this is true, and we have already been brought near to God, how then do we set our hearts on pilgrimage?

We might not have to make a physical pilgrimage to the temple in Jerusalem with animal sacrifices to commune with the Lord, but in the same way the physical sacrifices were a foreshadowing of a greater spiritual reality, so the physical effort/journey of an Old Testament pilgrim foreshadowed a greater spiritual reality of the Christian disciple.

In the Old Testament, God drew near to his people by placing himself in their midst—residing in the temple in the heart of Jerusalem. He then provided the Israelites access to his dwelling place through the conditions of the sacrificial system. This was grace. They had not earned God's proximity or his presence.

These privileges, afforded to them by grace, were only accessed through faith, however. If an Israelite didn't take advantage of the privileges by journeying to the temple and entering into its courts, the privileges were moot. It wouldn't matter if he were to live right next door to the temple, let alone hundreds of miles away, if he didn't put in the necessary effort to take advantage of such proximity and the access afforded to him by his Jewish heritage. Proximity and access don't equal God's presence or a relationship with him. Without pilgrimage, the privileges afforded by grace are nothing more than a missed opportunity.

The same is true with us. We have been justified for our sins. Therefore, *positionally,* we have been brought near to God. The Gospel has afforded us the grace of proximity and the opportunity to commune with God in an intimate relationship. But just because something is *positionally* true, that does not mean it has been *practically* taken hold of.

Allow me to explain further.

When I first met my wife Brittany, there weren't any fireworks or explosive chemistry between us. We are almost complete opposites. I'm social; she's shy. She's a thinker; I'm a feeler. I'm spontaneous; she's a planner. Nevertheless, despite the differences, the more we got to know one another, the more we fell in love.

We got married on April 30, 2016. It was one of the best days of our lives. We got to stand before the people most dear to us in this life and profess our love for one another. As we said our vows, committing ourselves in a covenant marriage to each other, the Bible says something profound occurred: we became one flesh (Genesis 2:24).

And, just like that, all our differences dissolved, and our communication issues were no more. As one flesh, we began to function in perfect synergy....

Not really.

As much as I wish that were true, that's not how it works, is it?

Positionally we became one flesh on our wedding day—meaning the Lord considers us one—but it will take a lifetime of *hard work* to truly learn to function as one. Chemistry, intimacy, love, and trust—all of these things—take time and effort, day in and day out; they don't just happen. Relationships don't work like that. We can't just rest in what is positionally true. In marriage, the husband and wife are either moving toward intimacy or moving away from it; there is no staying the same.

The same is true in our relationship with the Lord. As great as the differences are between my wife and me, the differences between God and us are much, much greater. He is holy, righteous, and perfectly loving; we are decidedly not. We won't just stumble upon the unsearchable depths of God's glory and love; it will take time and effort to grow in our relationship with him.

To set our hearts on pilgrimage is to wake up each day and set our proverbial GPS, with Jesus as the destination. It is to practically and appropriately re-orient the trajectory of our entire lives in pursuit of him. It is a spiritual journey to practically realize what is already positionally true.

We may not have to make a physical pilgrimage the way the Israelites of the Old Testament did, but we still have a spiritual pilgrimage to make—a journey marked by the same level of planning and preparation as the Old Testament pilgrim. It will take the same level of effort and intentionality as we strive and strain our way through the scorching valleys and tumultuous terrain of Christian discipleship. The differences between our pilgrimage and theirs is a matter of kind, but not of degree. Theirs was physical; ours is spiritual. But our hearts should be no less set on the courts of the Lord—we should have no less yearning to be in His presence than the psalmist in Psalm 84.

In Jeremiah 29, God's people have been sent into exile in Babylon because of the way they have continually broken their covenant with the Lord. Despite this, God offers them this promise:

> When seventy years are completed for Babylon, I will visit you, and I will fulfill to you my promise and bring you back to this place. For I know the plans I have for you, declares the LORD, plans for welfare and not for evil, to give you a future and a hope. Then you will call upon me and come and pray to me, and I will hear you. *You will seek me and find me, when you seek me with all your heart.* I will be found by you, declares the LORD.... (Jeremiah 29:10-14)

By the blood of Jesus, we have access to an even greater manifestation of this promise. We have been redeemed from our spiritual exile and brought into the heavenly Jerusalem. We now have unmitigated access to the Lord (Ephesians 2:18). How much more then do you think we will be able to find him if *we* seek him with all our heart?

VIII.

THE PURSUIT OF HOLINESS

The pursuit of holiness is perhaps the most important, yet the most neglected, matter in the church today. Apart from this pursuit, there is no revival in the church, personally or corporately. It is absolutely essential to discipleship, and its absence is the reason so many of us have stagnated spiritually.

1 Peter 1:14-16 instructs, "As obedient children, do not be conformed to the passions of your former ignorance, but as he who called you is holy, you also be holy in all your conduct, since it is written, "You shall be holy, for I am holy."

Even though the pursuit of holiness is a Biblical command for the follower of Christ, it has become a sort of "red-headed step-child" in our churches. We've bought the lie that we can somehow pursue Jesus without pursuing holiness.

But look at what Hebrews 12:12-14 (emphasis added) says: "Therefore lift your drooping hands and strengthen your weak knees, and make straight paths for your feet, so that what is lame may not be put out of joint but rather be healed. Strive for peace with everyone, and *for the holiness without which no one will see the Lord.*"

Holiness matters. And if we truly desire to follow Jesus and draw near to the Lord, we must regain a passion and a love for pursuing it. But what exactly *is* holiness? And *why* is striving after it so essential to seeing the Lord?

What is Holiness?

Holiness is defined as "the state of being holy."[17] This is a state that belongs to God alone. 1 Samuel 2:2 testifies, "There is none holy like the Lord; there is none besides you; there is no rock like our God." And Exodus 15:11 rhetorically asks, "Who is like you, O Lord, among the gods? Who is like you, majestic in holiness, awesome in glorious deeds, doing wonders?"

To be holy is to be "exalted and worthy of complete devotion as one perfect in goodness and righteousness."[18] Hebrews 7:26 explains this quality in relationship to Jesus: "For it was indeed fitting that we should have such a high priest (Jesus), holy, innocent, unstained, separated from sinners, and exalted above the heavens." 1 John 1:5 adds, "God is light, and in him is no darkness at all."

As 1 Peter 1:14-16 commands us to be holy because God is holy, it ought to be clear that this does not mean we too are to be "exalted and worthy of complete devotion." God alone is worthy of such worship and praise. Philippians 2:6-7 makes evident that even Jesus, "though he was in the form of God, did not count equality with God a thing to be grasped, but emptied himself, by taking the form of a servant." Rather, it is the words "perfect in goodness and righteousness" that we are to pursue. In Matthew 5:48 Jesus instructs, "You therefore must be perfect, as your heavenly Father is perfect."

As we hear these words, the first thing that often comes to mind is the word "obedience." Thus, we might naturally relegate any discussion about holiness to a legalistic adherence to the Lord's commands. This is a partial truth; obedience is important. That is why Peter begins his exhortation that we be holy with "As obedient children," and why Jesus says, "If you love me, you will keep my commandments" (John 14:15). *Mere* obedience is not enough, however.

God does not want *just* an outward adherence to his commands; he wants our whole person—our actions *and* our hearts. We see this plainly in the Sermon on the Mount (Matthew 5-7), as Jesus dissects several of the Ten Commandments to make clear the sin of the heart behind the action is the most important. He explains if you haven't murdered someone, yet you hate that person in your heart, you've already committed the same root sin in your heart that manifests itself in murder (Matthew 5:21-22). If you haven't committed adultery, yet you've looked lustfully at another man's wife, you've already committed the heart sin that manifests itself in adultery (Matthew 5:27-28). While the action has been restrained, the heart remains corrupted and, consequently, condemned.

This is why obedience to the law is an insufficient means to save us. Romans 3:20 makes this clear: "For by works of the law no human being will be justified in his sight." The law reveals to us God's holy standard of righteousness; it tells us how to restrain our behavior, yet it has no power to transform our hearts. We see this consistently throughout the Scriptures. Religious people like the Pharisees would outwardly obey the law down to the last detail, yet their hearts were filled with coldness, pride, and evil motives. They obeyed the letter of the law, yet broke the spirit of the law in every way. To this, Jesus rebuked, "Woe to you, Scribes and Pharisees, hypocrites! For you are like whitewashed tombs, which outwardly appear beautiful, but within are full of dead people's bones and all uncleanness" (Matthew 23:27).

Holiness is not just mere obedience; it is a transformed heart. It deals with both the outer *and* the inner man. Psalm 139:23-24 reads, "Search me, O God, and know my heart! Try me and know my thoughts! And see if there be any grievous way in me, and lead me in the way everlasting!" This is the heart posture of one who is in pursuit of holiness. It invites God to reveal internal sin as well as external, and to uncover sins like self-righteousness, pride, and spiritual haughtiness, as well as any other corrupt and perverted motives for obedience.

Put simply, holiness is obedience of the whole person—from heart to deed.

Why is Holiness So Essential?

There are two categories of holiness we need to delineate before moving forward. The first is Jesus' holiness that is imputed (credited or attributed) to us. We are not holy, not even close. That is the very reason Jesus had to die in our stead. Through his substitutionary death on the cross, he paid the debt for our unholiness, and his holiness has been imputed to us. God looks upon us and, for all intents and purposes, sees those of us who are covered by the blood of Jesus as holy and righteous.

The second category is what I expand upon in the rest of this chapter: it is the holiness that is concerned with our internal and external obedience—the holiness on the human responsibility side of the divine curtain. This is the holiness to which Peter and the author of Hebrews are referring.

Here the concern is not so much with the realization of perfect holiness, which quite honestly won't occur on this side of heaven, but rather with *our pursuit* of it. It is this pursuit that makes possible the attainment of the imputed holiness of Christ and enables grace to have full effectiveness in transforming us increasingly into his holy image.

1. <u>Pursuing holiness is essential to repentance</u>.

The prerequisite to us being credited with the holiness and righteousness of Christ is *repentance*.

Before Jesus began his public ministry, John the Baptist was sent to prepare the way (John 1:23). His message was simple: repent and be baptized so that you will be ready when the Lord appears to receive him. In Matthew 3:11, John the Baptist proclaims, "I baptize you with water for repentance, but he who is coming after me is mightier than I, whose sandals I am not worthy to carry. He will baptize you with the Holy Spirit and fire." Acts 19:4 further explains, "John baptized with the baptism of repentance, telling the people to believe in the one who was to come after him, that is, Jesus."

John's message was the necessary predecessor to Jesus, because without repentance, no one can receive him or the salvation that is through him. Jesus makes this point clear in Luke 13:3: "No, I tell you; but unless you repent, you will all likewise perish."

These passages further show that repentance is essential to salvation and the forgiveness of sins:

- Acts 3:19: "Repent therefore, and turn again, that your sins may be blotted out...."

- Acts 11:18: "When they heard these things they fell silent. And they glorified God, saying, 'Then to the Gentiles also God has granted repentance that leads to life.'"

- 2 Peter 3:9: "The Lord is not slow to fulfill his promise as some count slowness, but is patient toward you, not wishing that any should perish, but that all should reach repentance."

But what exactly does it mean to repent?

Repentance begins with conviction. This is the recognition that we are sinners—that we have rejected and rebelled against God, breaking his commandments and occupying the position over our lives meant for him alone. The next step is *remorse*. It matters little if we are made aware of our transgression yet we are ambivalent about this truth. Remorse is concern over our disobedience, resulting in the desire to rectify it. The final component of repentance is the tangible manifestation of this desire for *rectification*. This includes confession, asking God for forgiveness, and actively turning from all we are convicted of.

To actively turn *from* our sin means to actively turn *toward* the absence of it. This absence *is* holiness.

As we reorient our lives in pursuit of Jesus, we must grasp the importance of pursuing holiness. It is the very essence of what it means to repent of our sinful trajectory. Holiness is the antithesis of everything we repented of in salvation. Pursuing it is striving after that which is opposite of pride, autonomy, idolatry, unrighteousness, selfishness, and godlessness. We cannot turn from those things without turning toward that which is absent of those things. Thus, we cannot turn toward Jesus in repentance without turning from our sin and toward holiness.

Without pursuing holiness, we have not truly repented. This of course is problematic (to say the least), but it is also clarifying. We begin to see that, as the writer of Hebrews makes the statement, "Strive for...the holiness without which no one will see the Lord," he is being more logical than legalistic. He isn't saying we have to achieve perfection to be saved. What he *is* saying, though, is if perfection isn't our heart's desire, then we haven't really begun following Jesus in the first place.

With this in mind, let's continue.

2. Pursuing holiness is essential to relationship.

As we talk about this idea of pilgrimage as a journey in pursuit of holiness, I suspect that many will be apprehensive—perhaps even fearful. After all, haven't we already seen man's attempt at holiness play out? Didn't the Old Covenant Law reveal to us that our efforts are futile? Aren't we talking about exactly the thing Paul so strongly condemns in Galatians 5?

> For freedom Christ has set us free; stand firm therefore, and do not submit again to a yoke of slavery.... You are severed from Christ, you who would be justified by the law; you have fallen away from grace.... You were running well. Who hindered you from obeying the truth? This persuasion is not from him who calls you.... I wish those who unsettle you would emasculate themselves (Galatians 5:1, 4, 7-8, 12)!

These are incredibly strong words of rebuke. If that wasn't enough, Paul adds in verse 3 that anyone who attempts to be justified under the law is responsible for keeping the entire law and will be judged according to its full standards.

But look again at Ezekiel 36:26-27 (emphasis added): "And I will give you a new heart, and a new spirit I will put within you. And I will remove the heart of stone from your flesh and give you a heart of flesh. *And I will put my Spirit within you, and cause you to walk in my statutes and be careful to obey my rules.*"

Something is different because of Jesus, but it's not that attempting to walk in obedience will be excluded under the New Covenant. Rather, the difference is that these efforts will no longer be futile. In addition to giving us a new heart (inner transformation), God actually gives us *his* Spirit to *cause* us to obey!

Not only is there a precursor to us being credited with the holiness and righteousness of Christ (repentance), but there is also an immediate successor. At the moment of (true) repentance, as we turn from our sin back toward holiness, we are given the deposit of the Holy Spirit to help us in our pursuit. In John 14:15-18 Jesus explains, "If you love me, you will keep my commandments. And I will ask the Father, and he will give you another Helper, to be with you forever.... You know him, for he dwells with you and will be in you. I will not leave you as orphans; I will come to you."

This is what is so unique about the Christian pilgrimage: we are on a journey in pursuit of God and his kingdom, and yet the journey is not made by us alone; it is made in relationship with the very One we seek.

This is great news, for apart from the leading of the Holy Spirit, any attempts at obedience or righteousness will fail, and they will imprison and destroy us in the process. *We cannot, by our own power, become more Christ-like or produce the fruit of the Spirit* ("love, joy, peace, patience, kindness, goodness, faithfulness, gentleness, self-control" (Galatians 5:22-23)). At best we will become a legalistic, self-righteous Pharisee, and at worst we will become so disheartened, discouraged, and hard-hearted that we will turn away from Jesus completely. The journey is too arduous, the distance too great; we cannot survive it alone.

To pursue holiness without pursuing the person of Jesus is futile. It is also true, however, that to pursue the person of Jesus without the understanding and intention of it involving a pursuit of holiness is equally as futile. These two aspects of Christian discipleship are so intricately tied together that it is impossible to separate the two. 1 John 3:24 makes this clear: "Whoever keeps his commandments abides in God, and God in him. And by this we know that he abides in us, by the Spirit whom he has given us."

To better make sense of this, we must understand the nature of our newly forged relationship with Jesus via the Holy Spirit. We must grasp that "relationship" does not mean we are on equal ground with Jesus. Yes, we have a friend in Jesus. Yes, as the Firstborn of all creation, he is our Brother in the spiritual family into which we have been adopted. But he is more than that; he is Lord. So, in addition to the dynamics of a familial relationship with Jesus, we must also maintain a master-servant dichotomy. We cannot allow our understanding of grace to undermine a proper reverence for the Lordship of Christ. In Luke 17:7-10, Jesus highlights this point:

> Will any one of you who has a servant plowing or keeping sheep say to him when he has come in from the field, 'Come at once and recline at table'? Will he not rather say to him, 'Prepare supper for me, and dress properly, and serve me while I eat and drink, and afterward you will eat and drink'? Does he thank the servant because he did what was commanded? So you also, when you have done all that you were commanded, say, 'We are unworthy servants; we have only done what was our duty.'

In Matthew 11:29, Jesus furthers this sentiment as he instructs, "Take my yoke upon you, and learn from me." In Jesus' day, a yoke was commonly used to tether two oxen together so they could be steered to pull a cart or a plow, according to a farmer's leading. The yoke would fasten around the necks of the two animals to keep them adjoined and moving in the same direction. Without it, it would be nearly impossible to keep the oxen moving where the farmer intended for them to go. At any time, either of the oxen could attempt to go in a way of their own choosing, and this would render any efforts at plowing (or any other intended purpose) useless. With the yoke in place, however, the animals would be led exactly where their master wanted them to go.

The same is true of us in discipleship. As we're tethered to Jesus in relationship through the Holy Spirit, we don't get an equal say in where we go. Like an ox under the yoke of a farmer, wherever the Spirit leads, we go. Romans 8:5, 12-14 explains:

> For those who live according to the flesh set their minds on the things of the flesh, but those who live according to the Spirit set their minds on the things of the Spirit.... So then, brothers, we are

debtors, not to the flesh, to live according to the flesh. For if you live according to the flesh you will die, but if by the Spirit you put to death the deeds of the body, you will live. For all who are led by the Spirit of God are sons of God.

Galatians 5:16-17 adds: "But I say, walk by the Spirit, and you will not gratify the desires of the flesh. For the desires of the flesh are against the Spirit, and the desires of the Spirit are against the flesh, for these are opposed to each other, to keep you from doing the things you want to do."

If we are being led by the Spirit, we will be in pursuit of holiness because the Spirit is *always* seeking to gratify his own desires. 1 John 2:3-6 provides further understanding: "And by this we know that we have come to know him, if we keep his commandments. Whoever says "I know him" but does not keep his commandments is a liar, and the truth is not in him, but whoever keeps his word, in him truly the love of God is perfected. By this we may know that we are in him: whoever says he abides in him ought to walk in the same way in which he walked."

If we are not pursuing holiness then we are not abiding in the Spirit (the very entity through which we experience relationship with Jesus). Without the Spirit, we don't belong to him (Romans 8:9); we don't know him. Thus, relationship with Jesus cannot exist in isolation from the pursuit of holiness.

3.   Pursuing holiness is essential for sanctification.

There is a quote that is rather popular in our culture these days: "Strive for progress, not perfection." While this is a wonderful thought when it comes to eating healthy foods or losing weight, it is quite dangerous when it becomes our Christian motto.

When we strive for progress instead of perfection, we start out expecting to fail, giving ourselves permission to do so in the process. It's like a child who doesn't try in school, sports, or music because it won't hurt as badly if he fails. By curbing our expectations, we can curb the pain of disappointment and failure. But that's exactly the point: in our Christian walks it *should* hurt when we sin. It *should* hurt when we disobey God. God has purposes for this pain!

Consider King David. After he sinned by committing adultery with Bathsheba in 2 Samuel 11, the prophet Nathan confronts David with his sin. As he realizes what he has done, he is cut to the core by a deep, heart-level conviction. He is broken over the fact that he has sinned against his God. Out of this brokenness, David pens Psalm 51, where he cries out to the Lord in repentance. In verse 17, he professes "The sacrifices of God are a broken spirit; a broken and contrite heart, O God, you will not despise."

Acts 13:22 reads, "I have found in David the son of Jesse a man after my heart, who will do all my will." David was an adulterer and a murderer, and yet God calls him a man after his own heart. How can this be? It certainly wasn't that he was perfect. Rather, it was that when he did mess up it brought him to his knees. He had such a desire in his heart to seek God with all that he had that when he was unable to carry out all of his good intentions, it broke him.

The same is true of Peter, Jesus' most favored disciple. Peter tells Jesus he will follow him to prison or to death, but when the moment comes, he cowers and denies Jesus three times. He is unable to live up to the earnest desire he has to follow Jesus, whatever the cost. This broke him, and the Bible says he wept bitterly (Matthew 26:75).

Finally, Paul exhibits the same struggle in Romans 7:24 (NIV) as he proclaims, "What a wretched man I am!" in response to his inability to carry out the desire he possesses to do what is right and good.

When was the last time you were truly broken over your sin? When was the last time it caused you to weep bitterly or "beat your breast," as every fiber in you repented of your failure to "live a life worthy of the calling you have received" (Ephesians 4:1, NIV)?

THE IMPLICATIONS OF FAITH

Deep brokenness over sin characterized all three of the godly men I have just discussed. But that brokenness didn't just happen; it was the result of a heart that was so set on living a life fully surrendered to God—a life in an unceasing pursuit of holiness—that it was emotionally overwhelming to fall short. The love they had for their Savior, in response to God's love for them, was so great that it logically followed that they would set their hearts on a life that reflected this love. This is why Paul would "strike a blow to [his] body and make it [his] slave" (1 Corinthians 9:27, NIV), and why he urges us as believers to "run in such a way as to get the prize" (1 Corinthians 9:24, NIV) and to "throw off everything that hinders and the sin that so easily entangles" (Hebrews 12:1, NIV).

These men didn't strive for progress; they strove for perfection. They wanted to honor and glorify God in literally everything they did. It is because of *this* that when they fell short, it broke them. In their eyes, grace didn't excuse them from this pursuit; rather, it ran along with them to cover the gaps of what was lacking in their effort, to pick them back up when they fell, and to wrap them in the love of the Savior's arms when they began to question if they had sinned one too many times.

I have come to find that my soul is in its most peaceful, beautiful, and restful state when I am broken over my sin. It is in these moments that I truly see my own ugliness, sinfulness, unworthiness, and inadequacy apart from Christ. But it is also in these moments that God unleashes the floodgates of his mercy and grace and rains it down on me. It is in these moments where the words of Jesus on the cross, bloodied and battered as he proclaims with his last breath "It is finished," wash over me and begin to soften my calloused heart. It is in these moments that I truly understand it is by his wounds I am healed, that it is because he bore my sin (and its punishment) so that I could be credited with a righteousness not my own and be called a "child of God." It is in these moments that grace transforms me, and I emerge slightly more in his image—humble; worshipful; and with a heart full of love, mercy, and grace. Yes, I have come to find the conviction of the Spirit and genuine brokenness over my sin to be one of the sweetest places in all of life to be. It is in these moments that my strivings cease and my soul finds rest.

A broken spirit and a contrite heart are like a field that has been tilled; they are fertile ground ready to receive the dispensing of grace, that it might sprout up and grow into all fullness of holiness and maturity. This is why Matthew 5:3 states, "Blessed are the poor in spirit, for theirs is the kingdom of heaven." But the only way we experience this type of Gospel-saturated brokenness is if we pursue holiness as his word calls us. To start with an expectation of sin—to make no effort toward sinlessness—is to presume upon the grace of God, and, ironically, it prevents us from fully experiencing grace the way God intended. Just before Peter tells us in 1 Peter 1:13 that we are to be holy because God is holy, he tells us to set our hope fully on grace. You see, for Peter (and Paul and David), grace was never meant to be separated from a pursuit of holiness.

The Good News of Holiness

I understand that the topic of striving in pursuit of holiness is difficult for some. Many of us have been legitimately wounded by those who have preached justification by works, like the false teachers Paul so strongly condemns in Galatians 5, so it might be difficult to think of this chapter as good news. It might feel instead like an affront to the good news of grace and the freedom afforded to us by the Gospel. I understand that. But I promise you, when you really see holiness for what it is, you will see why that couldn't be further from the truth.

Pursuing holiness leads to true freedom.

God is a loving Father, but he is also a transcendent, sovereign Creator. This means he has our best interest in mind *and* he possesses the wisdom to know what is truly best for us. He created us, after all, and he created the world around us. Into this creation, he wove a sort of "natural law"—an innate right way to live and an innate wrong way to live. It was God's desire that we would not have to be faced with the anxieties of navigating these laws, but that we would remain blissfully ignorant, trusting God and living within God's creational intent for our lives. We simply were to live in relationship with him, enjoying him and sharing in his work of caring for Creation and exercising dominion over it, bringing glory to his name in the process. As for right and wrong, good and evil—that was God's business. As long as we stayed submitted to him, we needn't worry about anything else.

But then Adam and Eve were deceived into disobeying God, and as they ate of the fruit from the tree of the knowledge of good and evil, their eyes were opened to a complexity far beyond their capacity to properly navigate. Immediately following their disobedience, they experienced mental, spiritual, and emotional turmoil as a direct effect from living apart from God's creational intent and in contradiction to his natural law. For the first time, they experienced shame, guilt, selfishness, and fear in a way that God never intended. On top of this, their disobedience and departure from God's headship over their lives corrupted their nature so that their desire was no longer for good, but for evil. For the first time, mankind existed in a state of living outside of God's creational intent, and, with that, any clarity of how man was designed to live perished.

Sin spread like a noxious disease, so man was corrupted down to his core. Genesis 6:5 (NIV) explains, "The LORD saw how great the wickedness of the human race had become on the earth, and that every inclination of the thoughts of the human heart was only evil all the time."

As part of God's plan to redeem what was lost on that fateful day when Adam and Eve rebelled, he made a covenant through Moses with his people on Mount Sinai. God gave Moses Ten Commandments that served as a moral law, and another (approximately) six hundred "rules" that made up the ceremonial law (dealing with cleanliness, the sacrificial system, and providing further commentary on the full intent of the moral law). Israel's adherence to the law would result in God's blessing and their prosperity as a people, while their disobedience would bring about covenant curses.

But God's law was not arbitrary; what he commanded his people was not random. Rather, God, through his law, was giving insight into his creational intent. He was giving insight into the way he created the universe to function and his creation to function within that universe. The law, specifically the moral law, had always been true since the beginning of time. It was woven into the tapestry of Creation. God was just letting his people know so they would no longer make decisions that led to their own destruction, sickness, calamity, and death. Sin is a perversion of God's designed way for us to live. The law was given in love to guide God's people back into right living—to guide them back into what was truly best for them.

But why is this important?

The reason is this: the Gospel has reconciled us in relationship to God. He does not count our sin against us. He does not require from us the debt we have incurred, because Jesus paid the debt with his blood on the cross. For all intents and purposes, we are forgiven, redeemed, reconciled, and given the free gift of eternal life. Nothing can separate us from God, nor can we lose the salvation into which we have been brought. Thus, the Gospel nullifies the punishment for sin—the eternal consequences and our (eternal and temporal) separation from God in relationship. This is great news!

It does not negate the natural effects of sin, however. Sin is still a perversion of God's creational intent. Failing to live in complete surrender to the Lordship of Christ is still a perversion of God's creational intent. Before God punished Adam and Eve for disobeying him by expelling them from the Garden, they were "punished" by the natural effects of sin, as it (sin) resulted in an array of mental and emotional turmoil (fear, shame, selfishness, victim mentality, etc.). For the Christian, these natural effects will still be a "punishment" of sorts that continues to ravage our lives with turmoil until we decide in faith to put into practice what we claim to believe, living in light of the implications of our professed faith.

Imagine that God said it was a sin to walk off a cliff, but you decided to do so anyway. While grace means you would be forgiven for disobeying God, because of the natural law and God's creational intent, you would still suffer the "here and now" effects of the sin. Eternally, you would be secure—which is good because *you would die* from stepping off the cliff. Grace doesn't suspend the law of gravity.

Similarly, suppose you cheat on your wife, steal from a friend, lie to your boss, or get behind the wheel when you're drunk; will you not still suffer the consequences of these decisions? Does grace make pornography any less harmful in the way it rewires your brain? Does grace prevent pride and immaturity from leading to calamity? Every single sin under the sun has harmful ramifications, whether these ramifications are easily seen or not. Disobedience to God's commandments *always* has a damaging effect on the one who disobeys.

This isn't just true of that from which God tells us to abstain, but there are also negative effects for failure to do that in which God has called us to participate. If God told you to eat your vegetables and you disobey by not doing so, grace would mean you are forgiven for disobeying, but the natural effects of not getting the proper nutrients are still going to weaken your immune system and your overall health.

So whatever God has commanded us to do or not to do, it is for our good.

True freedom bought for us on the cross by the blood of Jesus is not the freedom to sin; it is the desire and ability not to.

In discipleship, we are submitting to the yoke of Jesus, following the Spirit toward holiness. But far from being the overwhelming, impossible-to-bear burden of legalism, Jesus promises, "My yoke is easy and my burden is light" (Matthew 11:30). 1 John 5:3 affirms, "And his commandments are not burdensome."

As he leads us, we can rejoice in knowing that what he commands us to do is actually what is best for us. It is actually what will give us the freedom, peace, joy, and contentment we had been seeking in going the way of our own choosing when we were slaves to our sinful nature. The Spirit is leading us to *life*.

Pursuing holiness as a Spirit-filled, grace-encompassed Christian is not burdensome; it is quite the opposite in fact. It is the only sure way to prosper us, not to cause us harm, to set us free, and to transform us increasingly into his holy image.

Grace doesn't free us from striving toward holiness; rather it changes our motivation for doing so. We do not do it to attempt to ascend to God, or to earn his love or our salvation. No amount of striving will ever accomplish these ends. Rather, we strive because he loves us, and this allows us to love in return. We understand that obedience is a tangible way to love God in return (John 14:15). We strive because we recognize the destructive nature of sin. We realize each and every sin is a rejection of and rebellion against the One who died to save us. We know we have been adopted by a Father who has our best interest in mind as he gives us guidance on what it looks like to live as a child of God. Finally, we understand that as we strive, fail (as we will inevitably do), and are broken by our sin, we will experience an outpouring of grace in a way that would be foreign to us otherwise. It is here that our striving truly ceases.

Dear Christian, I urge you: strive until your strivings cease. Love Jesus with your whole heart, mind, and soul. Strive for holiness, and let it bring you to your knees when you fall short, sweetly broken and wholly surrendered to his amazing grace.

CHAPTER 8 NOTES

[17] Dictionary.com, "Holiness," Accessed July 7, 2018. http://www.dictionary.com/browse/holiness.

[18] Merriam-Webster Online, "Holy," Accessed July 7, 2018. https://www.merriam-webster.com/dictionary/holy.

IX.

The Spirit to Guide You

A friend once said to me, "I want to surrender my life to Jesus; I'm just not sure what that looks like. How do I know what he wants me to do—what his vision for my life is instead of my own?"

The temptation is to think of surrendering our lives to Jesus and following after him in terms of "calling"; what does God want me to do with my life vocationally? We think that if we're surrendering the direction of our lives, our jobs, dreams, vision, time, money, etc. then that means all those things must necessarily change. Surrendering our lives (with our idols), however, doesn't mean we necessarily change all these things; it means we surrender control of them. We hold all things in an open hand. It means if Jesus does call us to change careers (or anything else for that matter), we'd be open to that possibility and obedient to seeing it through. Until then, we seek to glorify God in and through everything in our lives. The key in following Jesus is first and foremost a matter of the heart.

Nonetheless, there is a physical following of Jesus that must occur, but how do we do this?

In Jesus' day, this was a much simpler, more straightforward concept. When Jesus called his disciples (Matthew 4:19), the rich young ruler (Matthew 19:21), and the scribe (Matthew 8:20) to follow him, he meant literally to leave behind their lives and physically follow after him. Jesus was on the earth in the flesh. He was a person who went places, taught things, and did stuff.

But now it's not so easy to understand how we follow him. Yes, he has been raised from the dead and is alive, but his word tells us he is currently seated at the right hand of the Father in heaven (Acts 7:55-56, Romans 8:34, Ephesians 1:20, Colossians 3:1); he is no longer walking the earth in the flesh. So how do we follow him? How do we know where he's leading us to go? This is ultimately the question my friend wanted to answer: how do I follow an invisible God?

The answer is two-fold: the Spirit and the Word.

It is the symbiotic relationship between these two indispensable elements that enables us to clearly and effectively follow Jesus in faith on the journey of Christian discipleship. Thus, we will spend the next several chapters explaining how the Spirit and the word work together in perfect synergy to lead us on our journey.

A Life-Changing Revelation

I became a Christian the summer before my senior year of high school. Prior to that, I thought I was a Christian. I believed in Jesus intellectually, but it wasn't until that summer, while on a mission trip, that I surrendered my life to Christ.

My life immediately changed when I returned home from the trip. My language changed; what I was looking at on the Internet changed. I had a desire to read the Bible and learn more about Jesus, and I got involved in as many Bible studies and small groups as I

---

could. It was an amazing season of reprieve from the anxiety, depression, and sexual addiction (pornography) I had been dealing with for the years leading to my conversion. I was thoroughly enjoying my life's new direction.

As I headed to college, I felt God tug at my heart to go into ministry, so I found a small Christian university and enrolled in the Christian Education program. But something happened during the next several years. The fire faded; the depression, anxiety, and pornography returned. By the time I graduated, I was spiritually spent and completely burnt out. I didn't walk away from Jesus, but I did walk away from the idea of ministry.

Over the next couple of years after college, I continued to be faithfully committed to the routines and disciplines of the Christian life, but I felt as if something was missing. I was complacent, apathetic, and lukewarm.

Nonetheless, I continued the habit of regularly reading my Bible. One night, as I was reading the book of Acts, I came across a passage that would forever change my life.

On this particular night I was reading Acts 8:14-17 (NIV):

When the apostles in Jerusalem heard that Samaria had accepted the word of God, they sent Peter and John to Samaria. When they arrived, they prayed for the new believers there that they might receive the Holy Spirit, because the Holy Spirit had not yet come on any of them; they had simply been baptized in the name of the Lord Jesus. Then Peter and John placed their hands on them, and they received the Holy Spirit.

They had been baptized in the name of the Lord Jesus, but the Holy Spirit had not yet come on any of them? They were Christians, but didn't have the Holy Spirit? *That's it!* I thought, *That perfectly describes me! I know I'm saved, but something is missing!*

It was a revelation—an epiphany of epic proportions. I felt as if the Lord was speaking right to me, hitting me in the face with this new realization. I had been living a largely Spirit-less Christianity. I didn't know exactly what it meant, what to ask, or how to ask, but then and there, I got down on my knees and prayed, "God, I want your Holy Spirit. I want to be filled with it... or with more of it if I already have it. I want to be more aware of you, of it, of him! I don't know, God, I just want to be filled with your Spirit!"

I didn't speak in tongues; no flame or dove descended from heaven (that I could see anyway). But from that point forward, something was significantly and substantially different. Suddenly, the Scriptures came alive. God began illuminating verses and passages and writing them on my heart. He was giving me new understanding to things I had read a hundred times before.

Something divine occurs when knowledge about God moves from our heads into our hearts. I define it as the Wisdom of God—when head knowledge becomes life-changing. It is when the Holy Spirit takes what we know about God, writes it on our hearts, and we are forever changed. I was forever changed. God had poured out his Spirit on me and lit a passion and fire in me like I had never known before.

Now I realize there is something unique about the time in history in which that event in Acts 8 occurred. The Christians at this time were first-generation recipients of the Holy Spirit. It is possible that the Samaritans had been baptized into the name of the Lord before the Spirit had even been dispensed at Pentecost in Acts 2. They needed to hear about the Spirit from the apostles—to learn about him (the Holy Spirit) and know he had been given before they could receive him. Also, since the Samaritans were despised by the Jews, God wanted to make abundantly clear to the early church that the Spirit would not discriminate based on race or ethnicity; salvation had come even to the Samaritans who believed.

The circumstances in Acts were unique. I am not claiming that one can be a true Christian in the present day and not have the Spirit. Acts 2:38 explains, "And Peter said to them, 'Repent and be baptized every one of you in the name of Jesus Christ for the forgiveness of your sins, and you will receive the gift of the Holy Spirit.'"

I do believe, however, that we can have the Holy Spirit and not be aware of his presence. We can have the Holy Spirit and so quench him that there is no discernible evidence of his presence in our lives. Much in the same way that we are inclined to presume upon God's grace, we can presume upon the presence of the Holy Spirit. We view having the Spirit as our "right" as a Christian, but we have little understanding of who he really is. As a result, our faith isn't growing. We're frozen in spiritual immaturity because we've lost sight of our Guide—the very One we're supposed to be following on this pilgrimage.

This, of course, begs the question: how do we avoid this? How do we regain a Spirit-led Christianity?

First, we fervently and intentionally seek the Spirit as I have just mentioned, repenting of our neglect, ignorance, and presumptions regarding the third member of the Trinity, and praying that God in his grace would unreservedly restore in us that which we have forgotten. Next, we learn to expect, hear, discern, and obey the leading of the Spirit, and to posture our hearts with the type of humility and surrender that our position in Christ implies, making ourselves vessels for the Spirit to work in and through, according to his purpose and will.

The Leading of the Spirit

1. The Spirit Convicts

In the last chapter, I discussed how the Spirit desires holiness; thus, we can expect the Spirit will be leading us toward holiness. He does this not only by leading us toward righteousness and obedience, but also by revealing in us that which is unrighteous, calling us to repentance.

One of the primary functions of the Holy Spirit is to convict us (and the world around us) of sin. Jesus tells his disciples, "And when he comes, he will convict the world concerning sin and righteousness and judgment: concerning sin, because they do not believe in me; concerning righteousness, because I go to the Father, and you will see me no longer; concerning judgment, because the ruler of this world is judged" (John 16:8-11).

He does this prior to our conversion. The Holy Spirit opens our eyes to the fact that we are sinners deserving of hell and calls us to repentance and new life. But the conviction of the Spirit does not end with conversion; it is just the beginning.

Do you remember the movie *Shrek* when Shrek tells Donkey that ogres are complicated, like onions with many layers?[19] Well, people are like onions too; we have layers and layers of sin. When we surrender our lives to Christ, we are willfully resolving to surrender our sin as well, but we can't surrender something we don't see.

Often times there are a handful of sinful behaviors we are consciously aware that God is asking us to give up at the point of conversion. We may understand that "If I am going to become a Christian and follow Jesus, I can no longer steal from work and sleep with my girlfriend." But sin is far more pervasive than we sometimes realize; there are depths to our sin that take a lifetime to uncover. Thankfully, in his grace, God doesn't reveal the *entirety* of our sin to us all at once. Rather, bit by bit, layer by layer, he reveals more of our sins (behaviors, heart postures, idols, attachments, and addictions). By his grace, we are only responsible to repent of and surrender what he has revealed to us by his Spirit (this revelation can occur through the Bible, a Christian friend, a sermon, prayer, etc.). We are only responsible to maintain a clear conscience before the Lord (Acts 23:1; 24:16).

The Christian's journey is largely one of coming to a series of forks along the path as God reveals a new sin (or sin pattern) to us. At each fork, we can choose to ignore the Spirit's conviction and continue down the path of sin, or we can turn from that sin and continue in his grace in the way he is leading us. If we choose to continue in sin after the Holy Spirit has revealed it to us, we have left the narrow path and hindered further progress in our maturity and sanctification (not to say we have lost salvation, but we have diverged from the fullness of what Jesus died for us to take hold of in the here and now) until we repent. Thankfully, we have the Holy Spirit to make clear to us which way we should go each time we come to these forks in the road.

But *beware*, the further we walk down the path of sin, the further away the voice of the Spirit will seem. We will numb our conscience, harden our hearts, and smother the Spirit, making it increasingly difficult to hear his voice if we continue to ignore his conviction.

With each fork we come to, as we repent of our sin and continue with the Spirit down the narrow path, we begin to look more like Christ and grow increasingly closer to our desired destination. In the process, we grow more aware of the greatness of his mercy and his love for us.

We can be aware of our sin, but not broken by it. We can also be "broken" by the consequences of our sin (i.e., being broken that an affair led your spouse to leave you), but not actually by the fact that we have sinned against God. It is only when the Holy Spirit convicts us of our sin, when we are genuinely broken that we have sinned against our God, that our sin can be truly uprooted and eradicated. Thankfully, this is a primary function of the Holy Spirit.

2.   The Spirit Speaks to Us

For some of us, the idea that God speaks to us through the Holy Spirit is obvious; it is second nature. But for others of us, we might not be so sure. The idea that God speaks to us, other than through the Bible, is something with which we are not as comfortable.

The primary way God speaks to us is through the Word. This happens as the Spirit illuminates the Scriptures to give us a deep, heart-level understanding of his word that results in transforming the way we think and live. This is not a matter of merely intellectually learning what the Bible says; even non-believers, who don't possess the Spirit, are able to do that. Rather, when Spirit-filled believers read the Word of God, the Spirit intervenes, removing the veil from our eyes and revealing to us the mysteries of his wisdom and his Word. Apart from this intervention, we will gain head knowledge from the Bible, but not true understanding.

The Scriptures, however, are not the *only* way God speaks to us.

In the Bible, we see God speak to his people in a plethora of ways. He does so through the Scriptures and the preached Word, but other times he speaks in more "unorthodox" ways. He does so in dreams and visions, through angels and prophets, through a burning bush and a donkey, and in a gentle whisper following a storm.

Additionally, he does so through the internal leading and direction of the indwelling Holy Spirit. There is perhaps no better example of this than Jesus himself.

Immediately following Jesus' baptism, when the Holy Spirit descended upon him, we are told that the Spirit led Jesus out into the wilderness to be tested (Matthew 3:16-4:1). Here, we get a sense of what Jesus means when he says he can do nothing of his own accord, but only what he sees the Father doing (John 5:19). Jesus is being led in his earthly ministry by the Father, *through* the Holy Spirit. Despite having an inherent authority of his own, Jesus is being directed where to go, what to say, and what to do. He goes to the desert to fast and to be tempted because that's where the Spirit leads him to go. The Bible tells us this same Spirit lives in us (Romans 8:11).

Since we have been adopted as sons and daughters and credited with Jesus' righteousness, we have inherited his privileges, namely, the ability to have the same type of intimate relationship with the Father that Jesus did while he was here on earth. This includes being led on our pilgrimage by the Father, through the internal leading of the Spirit.

In the Spirit, we have a companion and guide as we set our hearts on pilgrimage and continue down the path of Christian discipleship. Every decision and every fork we come to, every proverbial leap of faith he is asking us to take, is not always a moral one, however. Obedience isn't always an issue of objective right or wrong. Sometimes the Spirit leads us to walk by faith regarding more personal and subjective decisions. Sometimes God is leading us to join *this* cause for the kingdom, or to specifically talk to *that* stranger; sometimes he will bring to mind a person or situation we know very little about to lift up in prayer. God may call us to walk away from a job, to move our family across the country (or world), or to give a portion of our money to a particular need. Whatever it is, if we're listening, God will continually lead us, day by day, moment by moment, in what it looks like for us to seek first the kingdom of heaven in our specific life circumstances.

It is hard to define the internal prompting and persuasion of the Holy Spirit, but this does not make it any less valid. The very concept of God intimately residing in us in the person of the Holy Spirit lends to the idea that we should expect he is speaking, directing, correcting, growing, and transforming us. We see this in 1 John 2:27: "But the anointing that you received from him abides in you, and you have no need that anyone should teach you. But as his anointing teaches you about everything, and is true, and is no lie—just as it has taught you, abide in him."

Do you feel how personal that is? The Spirit that you received *abides* in you and he will teach you all things.

The Gospel is that, in being redeemed by the blood of Jesus, we have also been reconciled with God to know him intimately and relationally. We no longer need priests and prophets as intermediaries between God and us. We have a Helper, Counselor, Teacher, and Guide dwelling inside us in the person of the Holy Spirit, leading and directing us; we just have to learn how to hear his voice.

Unfortunately, as many swing the pendulum away from the modern Charismatic Movement (a movement centered on the charismatic "gifts of the Spirit" (i.e., speaking in tongues, miraculous healings, prophecy, and the casting out of demons)), the idea that God speaks to us through the Holy Spirit, other than by his Word, has become a casualty. We have become so skeptical of even the slightest hint of the charismatic that we are missing out on one of the greatest blessings of the Holy Spirit: intimate, unabated communion and communication with the Father.

So what about the miraculous workings of the Spirit?

The book of Acts starts with a group of Jesus' followers gathered at Pentecost, praying and waiting for the promised Holy Spirit. In Chapter 2, the Spirit comes upon them like the "blowing of a violent wind" (verse 2), and with "tongues of fire" (verse 3), marking the beginning of the church on earth. By the power of the Spirit, the church begins to grow and spread at an unbelievable rate. Masses of people are converting to Christianity at once. Acts 2:41 tells of 3,000 people getting baptized into the name of Jesus by the power of the Holy Spirit in one day!

Not only was the Holy Spirit converting the hearts of sinners, bringing them from spiritual death to life, but people were also speaking in tongues, getting miraculously healed, casting out demons, and prophesying. These miraculous occurrences would come to be known as the "gifts of the Spirit"—a sure sign of the indwelling Spirit and a testimony to the legitimacy and the power of the Gospel message.

With the Spirit transcending the laws of nature in these ways, no obstacle could stand in the way of the spread of the church. Where the Spirit of the Lord was moving, it could not be thwarted. Acts 28:3-5 gives us a glimpse of this:

> When Paul had gathered a bundle of sticks and put them on the fire, a viper came out because of the heat and fastened on his hand. When the native people saw the creature hanging from his hand, they said to one another, "No doubt this man is a murderer. Though he has escaped from the sea, Justice has not allowed him to live." He, however, shook off the creature into the fire and suffered no harm.

Many of us hear these stories and cynicism immediately kicks in: "That stuff couldn't have actually happened. They just didn't know (scientifically) back then what we do now. There has to be another more reasonable explanation."

Or perhaps we would argue, "Of course God can do miraculous things, and he did. But those things were for then; God doesn't work like that anymore."

Whatever your inclination might be, these passages certainly do leave us with a few big questions: how does the Holy Spirit work today? Should we consider the miraculous ways the Spirit moved in the early church normative, or have some of these gifts of the Spirit (speaking in tongues, prophecy, healing, etc.) ceased?

There are two primary camps regarding the more miraculous workings of the Holy Spirit in the church today: the Cessationist and the Continuationist views. The Cessationist view contends the gifts have ceased. They existed for a time for the establishment of the early church and to verify the claims of the Gospel message, but died out with the apostles. Today, the Scriptures, the sacraments, and the structures established within the church are sufficient for the continued maintenance and expansion of the kingdom.

The Spirit works in more subtle ways now, giving wisdom, knowledge, understanding, spiritual new-birth, conviction of sin and repentance, encouragement, nourishment, and sustenance. The gifts of the Spirit are things like teaching, preaching, service, hospitality, and evangelism.

This position is based around a few key Scriptures. The first is Hebrew 2:3-4, which reads, "How shall we escape if we neglect such a great salvation? It was declared at first by the Lord, and it was attested to us by those who heard, while God also bore witness by signs and wonders and various miracles and by gifts of the Holy Spirit distributed according to his will."

The Cessationist argues the miracles and gifts existed for the purpose of attesting to and authenticating the revelation of the Gospel—the incarnation and the resurrection. Once that had been accomplished, the gifts ceased, as they were no longer necessary.

1 Corinthians 13:9-10 continues, "For we know in part and we prophesy in part, but when the perfect comes, the partial will pass away." The Cessationist argues from these verses that the Scriptures are the "perfect" that is said to be coming. In this view, instead of the perfect referring to the second coming of Christ, it refers to the completed, closed Canon (the Bible), which is entirely sufficient for all knowledge regarding Christ and salvation. Prophecies are not necessary, therefore, because all that is inspired prophecy has been recorded and preserved.

The second camp regarding this topic is the Continuationist view. The Continuationists contend there is no viable, Biblical evidence that would suggest the gifts have ceased. Instead, Paul seems to talk about the miraculous gifts as he lays out instructions for their use in the early church as if they are as commonplace to the indwelling of the Holy Spirit as any of the more "ordinary" giftings (teaching, leadership, hospitality, evangelism, etc.). They agree that 1 Corinthians 13:8-10 clearly expresses that certain gifts will cease when the "perfect" comes, but they contend this is obviously referring to the second coming of Christ. If the perfect has not yet come, there is little reason to expect the gifts to have ceased.

In addition, 1 Thessalonians 5:19-21 urges readers, "Do not quench the Spirit. Do not despise prophecies, but test everything; hold fast what is good." They point out that here Paul has the foresight to understand that many will try to deny the power and the work of the Spirit like the Cessationists seem to be doing. They will despise prophecies and quench the Spirit.

So what is the verdict? Have the gifts ceased?

First, let me say the verses I highlighted to support each position are in no way exhaustive. This is an incredibly complex debate, and I encourage you to study the Scriptures for yourself if you are uncertain about your position. I do believe, however, that fixating on this debate is perhaps to misplace our energies and efforts. Regardless of where you stand on the topic, I believe there is an absolutely crucial principle at play here regarding our relationship to the Holy Spirit, our willingness to let him lead us, and our ability to discern his voice.

The Bible talks about how a bad root produces bad fruit (Matthew 7:18). So, if there is bad fruit, might there be a bad root? Many of us have a hard time believing the Spirit can and does move in these ways because we haven't experienced it ourselves. But it is worth considering whether the lack of clear, undeniable expressions of the Spirit's power in our lives is evidence of a deeper issue. It is possible that we haven't experienced it precisely because we have closed ourselves to the possibility of the Spirit working in certain ways, hereby stifling the Spirit in the process.

The Bible urges us not to quench the Spirit (1 Thessalonians 5:19). It urges us not to treat prophecies with contempt (5:20) or to blaspheme the Spirit (accrediting to the Spirit what is not from him *OR* discrediting the Spirit of what *is* from him) (Mark 3:29). It also warns of a religion that seems spiritual but lacks power (2 Timothy 3:5). I believe we would do well to examine ourselves closely regarding such matters.

I fear that many of us do not experience the day-to-day leading of the Holy Spirit precisely because we refuse to surrender control to a Spirit the Bible says blows wherever he wills (John 3:8). Think about this: in Acts 2:13, as the Spirit falls upon the people at Pentecost, they begin to speak in tongues. What do the people observing them say? "These people are drunk! They're out of their minds!" I believe that if many of us are honest, we'd prefer the Spirit *not* work in or through us in a way that calls us beyond our comfort and control. We'd rather he not cause us to burst out in tongues like the people of Acts did because we would prefer not to look foolish or drunk (Acts 2:13) to the people around us. Or, what about in Acts 20, where we see the Spirit leading Paul to go to Jerusalem *despite* telling him that prison and suffering awaited him there? I believe we are erring on the side of denying the Spirit—of quenching and even blaspheming him—because we are afraid of what it might mean for us to surrender control.

"But, Craig, are you telling me I am to believe every reported 'miracle' by someone claiming to be filled with the Holy Spirit? What about the televangelists and their Hollywood productions and tent revival healings where the preacher proclaims, 'The power of Christ compels you!' as he smacks the ill or demon-possessed person in the forehead, at which point that person falls to the ground in convulsions? Or what about the people supposedly 'slain in the Spirit' who start barking like dogs, hysterically laughing, or spontaneously fainting?"

There is a Latin phrase that essentially translates to, "The abuse of some does not negate the proper use." I think this appropriately applies here. When we see people abusing the gifts and doing things in the name of the Lord that clearly aren't from him, things that aren't Biblical and detract from the Church's witness in the world, it can be tempting to swing the pendulum in the other direction. It is easier to deny the miraculous gifts and more charismatic workings of the Spirit. It is safer to put God in a box where we can predict what he's going to do. But the abuse by some people (and there are many people who are falsifying the Spirit for the sake of personal gain, attention, or even demonic purposes) does not negate the proper use.

Assuredly, we should not seek the miraculous gifts for selfish motives or as something we can wield in accordance with our own will; God dispenses the gifts as *he* wills. Not everyone will speak in tongues, heal, or prophecy. And even those who do shouldn't expect to be able to do so at will. Nonetheless, we should be open and expectant for God to move by all means necessary in order to accomplish *his* will.

It seems evident to me that the believer who opens himself up to be a vessel for the Holy Spirit to move through; who does not limit how, when, or in what ways he will move; and who does not quench the Spirit or treat prophecies with contempt—this person will experience Christ through the Holy Spirit in radical and powerful ways, both "ordinary" and miraculous.

Instead of denying the gifts and quenching the Spirit, we need to learn to test the spirits (as we will in the next chapter). This is how we can know if something is from a false spirit or if it is from *the* Spirit. Most importantly, this is how we can know with absolute certainty which way the Spirit is leading us on our journey.

Brothers and sisters, I cannot emphasize enough the essentiality of the Holy Spirit. Without the Holy Spirit as your guide, any and all efforts in pursuit of God and intimacy with him are in vain. There is no spiritual awakening or revival apart from the indwelling of the Holy Spirit.

The Holy Spirit is a precious gift—a deposit guaranteeing our salvation, and a Companion, Helper, Teacher, Counselor, and Guide.

But this gift must be intentionally sought and faithfully guarded. Pray for the Spirit—ask God for an awareness of him. I promise you, whatever your theological convictions, that God will not be offended if you intentionally pray for more of him, opening yourself up to be a vessel for him to move in and through.

_____

CHAPTER 9 NOTES

[19] *Shrek,* directed by Andrew Adamson and Vicky Jenson, (2001; Dreamworks, (2003) dvd).

X.

THE WORD TO GUARD YOU

1 John 4:1 instructs us, "Beloved, do not believe every spirit, but test the spirits to see whether they are from God, for many false prophets have gone out into the world."

The Holy Spirit is an incredible gift given to us to guide us in our pursuit of Christ. In him (the Spirit), we have the companionship of Jesus with us every step of the way along the often-arduous journey of Christian discipleship. He directs our every move—beckoning us, "This way. Follow me." It is a journey by faith as he leads and we follow.

But here's the problem: it's not just the Holy Spirit who's trying to lead us; there are many spirits—false spirits—who are attempting to lead us astray. So how do we know which Spirit is from God?

We test them, and we have been given *the* resource necessary to do just that.

The Bible tells us the same Spirit who raised Christ from the dead lives in us (Romans 8:11). This is the same Spirit Jesus promised would be sent to believers after he was crucified and rose again (John 14). It is the same Spirit who came upon the apostles at Pentecost (Acts 2:1-4) and to Paul on the road to Damascus (Acts 9). Most importantly, it is *the same Spirit* who inspired the writing of the Scriptures (2 Timothy 3:16).

1 John 4:2-3 (NIV) explains, "This is how you can recognize the Spirit of God: every spirit that confesses that Jesus Christ has come in the flesh is from God, and every spirit that does not confess Jesus is not from God. This is the spirit of the antichrist, which you heard was coming and now is in the world already."

In other words, we know the Spirit is from God if what he confesses and teaches falls in line with what we already know to be true—if it falls in line with who God is and how he acts in Scripture (i.e., In this instance, that Jesus is the Son of God who came to die on a cross for our sins so that whoever believes in him will have eternal life).

Conversely, if the spirit you are hearing is "teaching" you something, or leading you in a way that is counter to the truth, character, and nature of God as revealed in the Bible, then it is a false spirit sent by the enemy to lead you astray.

There is a great story by Max Lucado called *The Song of the King* that perfectly illustrates how we are to protect ourselves from being deceived by false spirits as we are led by the Spirit on our Christian pilgrimage. The story tells of a prince who offers a reward on the king's behalf to the knight who can successfully navigate his way through Hemlock Forest—a treacherous forest filled with menacing creatures called Hopenots—to the king's castle.

As the prince is describing the parameters of the challenge, he begins by explaining that each participant is allowed to select one companion to assist him on the journey. Next, he brings out a flute and begins to play a tune. He explains there is only one other flute like this one and it belongs to the king; the song is just as unique. The melody he has just played is the same one his father, the king, will play from his castle three times per day throughout the duration of the competition. To reach the castle, all they must do is follow the king's song:

The next morning the three knights mounted their horses and entered Hemlock. Behind each rode the chosen companion.

After many days and countless songs, a watchman spotted two figures stumbling out of the forest into the clearing. No-one could tell who they were. They were too far from the castle. The men had no horses, weapons, or armor....

....That evening a festive spirit filled the banquet hall. At every table people tried to guess which knight had survived Hemlock Forest. Finally, the moment came to present the victor. At the king's signal the people became quiet, and he began to play the flute. Once again the ivory instrument sang. The people turned to see who would enter. Many thought it would be Carlisle, the strongest. Others felt it would be Alon, the swiftest. But it was neither. The knight who survived the journey was Cassidon, the wisest.

"Tell us of your journey," he was instructed. The people leaned forward to listen.

"The Hopenots were treacherous," Cassidon began. They attacked, but we resisted. They took our horses, but we continued. What nearly destroyed us, though, was something far worse."

"What was that?" asked the princess.

"They imitated."

"They imitated?" asked the king.

"Yes, my king. They imitated. Each time the song of your flute would enter the forest, a hundred flutes would begin to play. All around us we heard music—songs from every direction."

The king asked the question that was on everyone's lips. "Then how did you hear my song?"

"I chose the right companion," he answered as he motioned for his fellow traveler to enter. The people gasped. It was the prince. In his hand he carried the flute.

"I knew there was only one who could play the song as you do," Cassidon explained. "So I asked him to travel with me. As we journeyed, he played. I learned your song so well that though a thousand false flutes tried to hide your music, I could still hear you. I knew your song and I followed it."[20]

Cassidon learned the king's song so well that he knew which tune was false and which was true. Jesus tells a similar parable in John 10:1-5 (NIV):

I tell you the truth, the man who does not enter the sheep pen by the gate, but climbs in by some other way, is a thief and a robber. The man who enters by the gate is the shepherd of his sheep. The watchman opens the gate for him, and the sheep listen to his voice. He calls his own sheep by name and leads them out. When he has brought out all his own, he goes on ahead of them, and his sheep follow him because they know his voice. But they will never follow a stranger; in fact, they will run away from him because they do not recognize a stranger's voice.

Do we know the voice of our shepherd so well that we can discern his voice from that of the enemy? Do we know his voice so well that we will run to follow him but run from any voice that is not from him? We need to, and this is how we do it: we get in the Word, and we meditate on it day and night. We immerse ourselves in it. God has two flutes: the Spirit and the Word, and they *always* play the same tune.

The Bible is the inerrant, authoritative, inspired word of God. It is not merely a book written by man about God; it is a book written *by* God *through* man *under* the divine inspiration of the Holy Spirit. When interpreted correctly, in the right context, it is without error. Since God is the same yesterday, today, and forever, his word is time-less. It is just as relevant and applicable today as it was two thousand years ago.

Do you believe this? Before you continue reading, I encourage you to answer this question for yourself. What we believe about the Bible is arguably the most important decision we will ever make re-garding our Christian faith. To this point, Adrian Rogers tells this sto-ry of Billy Graham:

> In 1949, when Billy Graham was a very young man, he harbored the same doubts about the Bible that many young people have. When he stood up to preach, there was a lack of power. He knew an intel-lectual battle was waging in his mind over the authority of God's Word. That year God allowed him to spend some time in the moun-tains outside Los Angeles. There he wrestled with God and with himself. He said, "In desperation, I surrendered my will to the living God revealed in Scripture. I knelt before the open Bible and said, 'Lord, many things in this book I do not understand, but thou hast said the just shall live by faith. All I have, I have received by faith. Here and now by faith, I accept the Bible as thy Word; I take it all; I take it without reservations. Where there are things I cannot un-derstand, I will reserve judgment until I receive more light. If this pleases thee, give me authority as I proclaim thy Word, and through that authority convict me of sin and turn sinners to the Savior.'"

> Within six weeks of that prayer, Billy Graham preached the great Los Angeles crusade where thousands were swept into the kingdom of God. His ministry caught on fire for the Lord—making a global impact for the Savior! Now, he recognized that he didn't have to prove the Bible was true. He had settled it in his mind, and that faith impacted his preaching and the men and women who were saved as a result. Now he had a quick, powerful weapon in his hand—a two-edged sword that could pierce the hearts of people. He had a

flame with which to melt away the unbelief of people, a hammer to break up the stony covering of hearts. All this, Billy Graham says, is why, to this day, he frequently begins sentences with the phrase, "The Bible says..."21

If we don't believe the Bible is the word of God and is trustworthy, how can we follow Jesus in faith? Rarely, if ever, will we be confronted by a crisis of faith, because any passage or verse calling us to something we deem too costly, too uncomfortable, or too disagreeable, we will ignore instead of humbly submitting to the idea that God must know something we do not. We will simply follow a way of our own choosing, adhering to what we like about the Bible and discarding the rest. But faith requires we follow the way of *his* choosing, and he has made this way known through the Bible.

What we believe about the Bible, and whether we are regularly immersing ourselves in it, is absolutely essential to the Spirit-led Christian life.

Now, some people might go too far and argue the *only* way God speaks to us is through Scripture, and only by teaching us about Jesus or convicting us of sins. While this is a large part of how he speaks to us, we must be very careful here. Not only does this neglect a great deal of evidence of the Spirit's leading in the Bible, but it also runs the risk of making the Spirit into a sort of "Jack-in-the-Box": if we want to experience him, we have to open the Bible because that is where he lives. But this is not accurate; the Spirit lives in *us*! *We* are the temples of the Holy Spirit (1 Corinthians 6:19), and he is ever leading us to walk in his ways.

The Holy Spirit is extra-Biblical; this means we can have a dynamic relationship with the living God on a moment-to-moment basis. He can speak to us in any number of different ways, from internal promptings to the lyrics of a song we hear on the radio. Through the Spirit, we can experience God anytime and anywhere with full, relational intimacy. In order for this to occur, however, we have to know how to discern his voice from all the false voices, and we can only do this if we are deeply proficient in his Word!

The Holy Spirit is extra-Biblical, but he is never counter-Biblical. 1 Corinthians 12:3 says, "Therefore I want you to understand that no one speaking in the Spirit of God ever says 'Jesus is accursed!' and no one can say 'Jesus is Lord' except in the Holy Spirit." The Spirit will always speak in accordance with the truth of God's Word. He will *never* lead you in a way that is counter to scripture, that puts your hope in something other than the Gospel, or that by word or deed, says anything other than "Jesus is the Lord of my life."

This truth also applies to our discussion on the miraculous gifts. Let's take, for example, the gift of speaking in tongues. In 1 Corinthians 14:27-28 Paul instructs, "If any speak in a tongue, let there be only two or at most three, and each in turn, and let someone interpret. But if there is no one to interpret, let each of them keep silent in church and speak to himself and to God." Thus, if there is chaos or pandemonium as a church filled with people are all speaking in tongues, barking, etc., that is clearly in contradiction to the Bible's teaching of who God is and how he moves. We are able to test the spirits in those situations because we know from his Word the way in which tongues ought to be expressed in church.

In 1 Corinthians 14, Paul affirms the gift of tongues by saying he wishes that everyone spoke in them as much as he does (v. 5). But then he puts them in their proper order of importance by explaining that there are gifts far more important and implores us to seek these greater gifts (v. 12). Finally, he gives us instructions on how the gift of tongues is to function (v. 27-28). This provides us with a backdrop to test the spirits against. It enables us to accurately discern a healthy, Biblical expression of the Spirit from false expressions without throwing the "baby out with the bath water." We can have a heart posture toward God that is open and expectant for the Spirit to move in supernatural ways without believing every "spirit" that claims to be from God.

Christian, are you deeply rooted in God's Word? You have been given the deposit of the Holy Spirit—the indwelling of the Living God—to lead you, guide you, teach you, and give life to what was once dead. But apart from this essential element of the Christian faith (deep-rootedness in God's Word), you will not be able to experience the blessing of the Spirit's indwelling because you will not be able to discern the voice of Jesus from the multitude of false voices seeking to lead you astray. The Bible is the supreme authority for the truth and character of God. It is *the* way we learn to discern his voice!

As you embark on this pilgrimage, you too will be attacked by the vicious and cunning *Hopenots* seeking to lead you off course, away from your destination, and to disastrous ends. Thankfully, in Christ, we already have the right Companion; now it's up to you to make sure you know his song.

CHAPTER 10 NOTES

[20] Taken from *The Song of the King* by Max Lucado, © 2000, pp. 20-31. Used by permission of Crossway, a publishing ministry of Good News Publishers, Wheaton, IL 60187, www.crossway.org.

[21] Adrian Rogers, *The Incredible Power of Kingdom Authority*, (B&H Publishing Group, Nashville, 2002), 133-134. Excerpt used by permission, all rights reserved.

XI.

A Secret Wisdom

There is another way we are able to know God's will for our lives. Romans 12:2 tells us, "Do not be conformed to this world, but be transformed by the renewal of your mind, that by testing you may discern what is the will of God, what is good and acceptable and perfect." That sounds great, doesn't it? But what does it mean?

Here, Paul, the author of Romans, is talking about worldview. Worldview is essentially the lens through which we see the world. This lens becomes the agent through which we analyze and interpret all life and its happenings. Consequently, it shapes the course of our day, determines what we value and pursue, and informs us whether the circumstances we find ourselves in are "good" or "bad." Essentially, it is the ideological epicenter from which all our actions and emotions flow.

The movie *National Treasure* provides a helpful illustration. In the movie, Ben and his colleagues are in pursuit of a hidden treasure—one in which they believe there to be a map for on the back of the Declaration of Independence. Upon gaining access to the Declaration of Independence, they discover there is no map—at least not one they can see with the naked eye. They begin to hypothesize it is written in invisible ink.

As the movie progresses, Ben discovers an ocular device (a specialized pair of spectacles) that allows him to read the map drawn in invisible ink. The spectacles have layers of colored lenses: a clear layer, and then blue, red, and green lenses as well. Each layer by itself only reveals part of the map, and the wrong combination of lenses will point them toward the wrong destination; only the right combination of the lenses will accurately show them the path to the treasure.[22]

This is similar to what Paul is explaining in Romans 12:2. If we want to know what God's will is for our lives—how we should live, what we should do, and where we should go—we are going to need the right lenses. We will need to replace our worldly lenses with spiritual ones. We need to fundamentally alter the way we see and understand everything—the basic ideologies, principles, and wisdoms that have been ingrained in us as common sense and universally true since birth.

In order for this to make sense, we must understand the ideologies of the world and the kingdom of heaven are fundamentally and diametrically opposed. Does that sound drastic? It ought to, for it is no small thing to be brought from spiritual death to eternal life—from life as a prisoner to one who has been set free.

It should come as no surprise that God has a different perspective from ours because his is not hindered by the same limitations; it is an eternal perspective. He alone existed before time began and created all things by his word and the work of his hands. He alone knows the details of his will for the future, understanding without exception how we ought to live—what does and does not matter.

In Isaiah 55:9-10 God declares:

For my thoughts are not your thoughts,
neither are your ways my ways, declares the LORD.
For as the heavens are higher than the earth,
so are my ways higher than your ways
and my thoughts than your thoughts.

In 1 Corinthians 3:18-20, Paul explains, "Let no one deceive himself. If anyone among you thinks that he is wise in this age, let him become a fool that he may become wise. For the wisdom of this world is folly with God. For it is written, 'He catches the wise in their craftiness,' and again, 'The Lord knows the thoughts of the wise, that they are futile.'"

And Luke 16:15 (NIV) adds, "What people value highly is detestable in God's sight."

Listen to some of the ways the wisdom of God differs from the wisdom of man:

- If you want to be first you must become last (Mark 9:35)
- If you want to become great you must become a servant (Matthew 20:26)
- If you want to live you must die (Luke 9:24)
- To die is gain (Philippians 1:21)
- Count it as joy when you suffer (James 1:2)
- It is better to give than to receive (Acts 20:35)
- Do not store up for yourselves treasure on this earth (Matthew 6:19)
- Love your enemies (Matthew 5:44)
- Pray for those that persecute you (Matthew 5:44b)
- Forgive those that have wronged you (Matthew 6:12, 14)
- Turn the other cheek (Matthew 5:39)
- When you are weak you are strong (2 Corinthians 12:10)
- Do not fear what they fear (1 Peter 3:14)

- Do not fear those that kill the body (Matthew 10:28)
- Share in suffering as a good soldier of Christ Jesus (2 Timothy 2:3)
- Give out of your poverty (Mark 12:44)
- Do not worry about what you will eat, drink, or wear (Matthew 6:25)
- Lead by serving (Mark 9:35, Philippians 2:7)

Plain and simple, God is looking at things through a different lens than we do. So then, how do we change our lens and gain *his* perspective?

To some degree, we are powerless to change our worldviews. The Bible tells us that sin has distorted our perception of reality; it has caused a spiritual blindness. The effect is that we are (or were, prior to salvation) ever seeing but never perceiving, ever hearing but never understanding (Matthew 13:14, Isaiah 6:9). In other words, regardless of what is in front of us, we are unable to interpret it correctly because we are seeing it through the wrong lens. A veil has been placed over our hearts and minds so that we cannot see, know, or understand truth. To change our worldviews, then, requires the removal of this veil from our eyes, so that we see more clearly what is real and true. Since "you don't know what you don't know" and "the blind can't lead the blind," this requires we be acted upon by an outside force—one who is not blind; it requires a Savior.

The Greek philosopher, Plato, has a well-known illustration called "The Allegory of the Cave" [23] that I find quite helpful for understanding the fundamental worldview shift brought about (or at least that ought to be brought about) by our salvation and subsequent sanctification. In the story, he asks the reader to imagine there is a group of people deep within a cave, chained to the ground in the middle of it, facing a wall opposite the entrance. Having been there since birth, they know of nothing outside it. They don't even know they are prisoners, for they are unaware an alternative (freedom) exists.

There is a fire behind the prisoners that illuminates the wall they are facing, and every day, their captors march puppets in front of the fire, projecting shadows of animals and people onto the wall. Not knowing the origin of the shadows is the puppets (for their chains prevent them from seeing what is behind them), the imprisoned people deem the shadows themselves to be what is real. Naturally, this becomes the focal point of their existence.

These shadows are their only stimuli, their only entertainment, and their only opportunity to demonstrate skill. So they name the creatures and compete with one another to see who can most quickly and correctly identify the most shadows. This becomes their way of differentiating between one another, allowing them to create rankings and social classes. They celebrate the one who is the most skilled at this activity and make him their leader. After all, he is the most talented person at the most important thing in all their existence.

To the prisoners of the cave, the shadows are everything, for in them is the meaning of life.

Now imagine for a moment that one of the captives was set free from his chains, forced up the long, winding path, and thrust out of the cave entrance into the open air. True, at first he might experience more than a little discomfort from exercising his underdeveloped muscles after a lifetime of inactivity, as well as from the brightness of the sunlight to eyes that have never seen anything but the dimness of a cave. But imagine what it would be like as his eyes begin to adjust, and he sees creation in all its radiant beauty for the first time—rivers and fields, green grass and blue skies, trees, birds, and butterflies! It would all seem so amazing, and in an instant that man's worldview would be forever changed. In light of the magnificent beauty in front of him, never again would the shadows of puppets cast on the wall of a dimly lit cave carry any significance in his life. This man would have "died" to the false reality of the cave.

When all the man knew were shadows, the shadows had an immense amount of influence on his worth, happiness, and contentment. Did he perform well during the competition? Was he able to correctly and quickly identify all the shadows? Did he earn the praise, respect, and admiration of his peers by his performance? If not, it would be crushing, as if the world had ended; nothing in the world could be worse. But after being set free from the cave, he would see how insignificant the shadows were; how futile were the activities of his former way of life in the cave. What once seemed big and important would suddenly seem small and not so important. As Plato explains it:

> Then if he called to mind his fellow prisoners and what passed for wisdom in his former dwelling place, he would surely think himself happy in the change and be sorry for them. They may have had a practice of honouring and commending one another, with prizes for the man who had the keenest eye for the passing shadows and the best memory for the order in which they followed or accompanied one another, so that he could make a good guess as to which was going to come next. Would our released prisoner be likely to covet those prizes or to envy the men exalted to honour and power in the cave? Would he not feel like Homer's Achilles, that he would far sooner "be on earth as the hired servant in the house of a landless man"[24] or endure anything rather than go back to his old beliefs and live in the old way?

> Yes he would prefer any fate to such a life.

> Now imagine what would happen if he went down again to take his former seat in the cave. Coming suddenly out of the sunlight, his eyes would be filled with darkness. He might be required once more to deliver his opinion on those shadows, in competition with the prisoners who had never been released, while his eyesight was still dim and unsteady; and it might take some time to become used to the darkness. They would laugh at him and say that he had gone up only to come back with his sight ruined; it was worth no one's while even to attempt the ascent. If they could lay hands on the man

who was trying to set them free and lead them up, they would kill him.[25] Yes, they would.[26]

So then, the freed man's wisdom, which was true wisdom from above, would be foolishness to the prisoners because it dealt with things they could neither see nor understand. It would be as if it were a "secret wisdom." Meanwhile, the prisoners' wisdom, what they valued and felt was important, would be foolishness to the freed man.

So we see how a perspective change fundamentally alters what we value and how we see the world in which we live. The freed man had his mind renewed from the finite, limited perspective of a prisoner in a cave, to that of a free man who now understands the light and life above, and he is transformed by it. Only now can he accurately discern what is good, important, and worthwhile.

The Bible tells us that we too were born into a proverbial cave and held captive as prisoners to our sinful nature, unbeknownst to us. We too were deceived into consuming ourselves with shadows— mere illusions of reality. We too were deceived into putting value in things that had none, and as our Savior sets us free from our chains and opens our eyes to a beauty (and an eternal kingdom) the likes of which we have never seen before, we too become enlightened to the false reality of the world and its ideologies that have deceived and imprisoned us for so long.

The Gospel necessarily changes everything about how we see the world, how we live, and what we deem important. There is a quote by an unknown author that says, "We lose our addictions to lesser affections by being captivated by greater affections." As we fix our eyes upon the immeasurable beauty, magnitude, and sufficiency of Christ and eternal life in him, it ought to change the very lens through which we see the world.

Now some of you are perhaps apprehensive that I would rely so heavily on an allegory from Plato in this chapter, and understandably so. Plato was not a Christian (he lived 400 years before Christ), nor was he Jewish, so what could he possibly teach us about Jesus, the Bible, or the Christian faith? First, allow me to say, I am not espousing Plato and all his philosophies. To be honest, I have read very little of his writings outside of this allegory. I am not advocating for a Neo-Platonistic Christianity.

I do believe, however, that all truth is God's truth. What I mean is, if an atheist proclaims, "Jesus is Lord," it is true regardless of the fact that the man who said it is an atheist. Furthermore, if I use a movie with redemptive themes and Biblical parallels (i.e., Superman) to illustrate a point during a sermon, it does not matter what the message of the director's other movies is, nor what his personal beliefs are; the truth of the parallel used in the illustration stands. Truth is truth regardless of the source, so wherein we can draw illustrations that assist us in understanding Biblical truth more clearly and deeply, we ought to do so. In this particular situation, I believe Plato's "Allegory of the Cave" is immensely helpful in understanding what Paul means in Romans 12:2 when he says we should be transformed by the renewing of our minds. The allegory demonstrates an uncommon understanding of wisdom as a construct—how it originates, what governs it, and its effect on our worldviews. Plato understood the "equation" for wisdom and its implications perhaps better than most Christians; he was simply missing the key "variable." He writes:

> In the world of knowledge, the last thing to be perceived and only with great difficulty is the essential Form of Goodness. Once it is perceived, the conclusion must follow that, for all things, this is the cause of whatever right and good; in the visible world it gives birth to light and to the lord of light, while it is itself sovereign in the intelligible world and the parent of intelligence and truth. Without having had a vision of this Form no one can act with wisdom, either in his own life or in matters of state.[27]

In other words, Plato understood true wisdom requires a "true north." It requires a fixed point by which all other points are measured, calibrated, and interpreted. Once identified and rightly understood, all wisdom can be discerned based off this point. What Plato didn't know was what, or rather who, that point was. He called it the essential Form of Goodness. The Bible tells us His name is Jesus:

> For since, in the wisdom of God, the world did not know God through wisdom, it pleased God through the folly of what we preach to save those who believe. For Jews demand signs and Greeks seek wisdom, but we preach Christ crucified, a stumbling block to Jews and folly to Gentiles, but to those who are called, both Jews and Greeks, *Christ the power of God and the wisdom of God* (1 Corinthians 1:21-24, emphasis added).

It is possible that Paul had Plato and his "Allegory of the Cave" in mind as he wrote his first letter to the church in Corinth. After all, Corinth was a cultural epicenter for Greek philosophy, and Paul demonstrated on multiple occasions a fluency in the popular philosophies of the day. He certainly would have been familiar with the "Allegory." Regardless, Paul informs us that Christ and him crucified is the fixed point (the essential Form of Goodness) that Plato had discussed. *He* is the point by which all wisdom is determined and shaped, the point from which all wisdom and knowledge flow. Jesus *is* the wisdom of God.

But here is what is interesting: in 1 Corinthians 2:6-16, Paul draws a distinction between the wisdom of the cross and what he calls a "secret wisdom" that is reserved for the mature:

> Yet among the mature we do impart wisdom, although it is not a wisdom of this age or of the rulers of this age, who are doomed to pass away. But we impart a secret and hidden wisdom of God, which God decreed before the ages for our glory. None of the rulers of this age understood this, for if they had, they would not have crucified the Lord of glory. But, as it is written,
>
> > "What no eye has seen, nor ear heard,
> >   nor the heart of man imagined,
> > what God has prepared for those who love him"—

these things God has revealed to us through the Spirit. For the Spirit searches everything, even the depths of God. For who knows a person's thoughts except the spirit of that person, which is in him? So also no one comprehends the thoughts of God except the Spirit of God. Now we have received not the spirit of the world, but the Spirit who is from God, that we might understand the things freely given us by God. And we impart this in words not taught by human wisdom but taught by the Spirit, interpreting spiritual truths to those who are spiritual.

The natural person does not accept the things of the Spirit of God, for they are folly to him, and he is not able to understand them because they are spiritually discerned. The spiritual person judges all things, but is himself to be judged by no one. "For who has understood the mind of the Lord so as to instruct him?" But we have the mind of Christ.

What then should we say is this secret wisdom?

In order to answer that question, we will return to the "Allegory of the Cave" one final time:

Now consider what would happen if their release from chains and the healing of their unwisdom should come about in this way. Suppose one of them set free and forced suddenly to stand up, turn his head, and walk with eyes lifted to the light; all these movements would be painful, and he would be too dazzled to make out the objects whose shadows he had been used to see. What do you think he would say, if someone told him that what he had formerly seen was meaningless illusion, but now, being somewhat nearer to reality and turned toward more real objects, he was getting a truer view? Suppose further that he were shown the various objects being carried by and were made to say, in reply to questions, what each of them was. Would he not be perplexed and believe the objects now shown him to be not so real as what he formerly saw?

Yes, not nearly so real.

And if he were forced to look at the fire-light itself, would not his eyes ache, so that he would try to escape and turn back to the things which he could see distinctly, convinced that they really were clearer than these other objects now being shown to him?

Yes.

And suppose someone were to drag him away forcibly up the steep and rugged ascent and not let him go until he had hauled him out into the sunlight. Would he not suffer pain and vexation at such treatment, and, when he had come out into the light, find his eyes so full of its radiance that he could not see a single one of the things that he was now told were real?

Certainly he would not see them all at once.

He would need, then, to grow accustomed before he could see things in that upper world. At first it would be easiest to make out shadows, and then the images of men and things reflected in water, and later on, things themselves. After that, it would be easier to watch the heavenly bodies and the sky itself by night, looking at the light of the moon and stars rather than the Sun and the Sun's light in the day-time.

Yes, surely.

Last of all, he would be able to look at the Sun and contemplate its nature, not as it appears when reflected in water or any alien medium, but as it is in itself in its own domain.

No doubt.

And now he would begin to draw the conclusion that it is the Sun that produces the seasons and the course of the year and controls everything in the visible world, and moreover is in a way the cause of all that he and his companions used to see.[28]

For the prisoner set free from the cave, at what point should we say the man was no longer a prisoner? When his chains were removed? Yes, this would be the moment he was saved or set free (at least in the most basic sense), but at what point does he possess the ability to rightly discern all things (true wisdom)? Isn't it not until he can look fully upon the sun?

But what if once set free from his chains, the man were to just sit right back down in the place where he had been? What if he never makes the ascent out of the cave? Does he now differ from the person sitting next to him? The answer would be both quite a lot and very little. He differs in that he is no longer bound by chains, which is no small distinction, and yet his worldview would be nearly the same as those next to him who were still bound by chains. Would he not still value the shadows? Would his eyes not still be adjusted to the darkness? Would he still not be imprisoned by his ideologies—lacking true wisdom and unable to rightly discern the meaning or importance of things?

I tell you the truth, even if he were to read *every* book written by every person who had looked upon the sun—even if the sun itself were to write a book of its own description—as long as the man stays in the cave, he will not yet understand as he ought. His eyes will be no more adjusted to the light, still every bit conformed to the darkness. No, in order to truly understand, the man must experience the ascent himself. He must endure the pain of his eyes adjusting from the dark to the light himself. He must have his understanding of the cave, the shadows, and the puppets deconstructed by seeing beyond them for himself. Finally, he himself must stare upon the sun with eyes fully adjusted before he can return to the cave fully transformed.

The man from the "Allegory" *does* make the ascent, and, as he returns to the cave, he now possesses the secret wisdom. That is, he has looked upon the sun, and only because of this does he rightly understand everything else. He may have been free prior to that, but his wisdom was incomplete.

Every analogy, if taken far enough, eventually breaks down; but here is the point: grace is just the beginning, not the end. Don't hear what I am not saying; we never graduate beyond our need for God's grace. But we are not forgiven for the sake of being forgiven. We are forgiven to be reconciled, redeemed, and restored. The Gospel removes a veil and sets us free from our chains, but we do not yet see as we ought. Instead, the journey of sanctification, of being transformed by the renewing of our minds, has just begun. By looking upon the Son, we have the ability to see God in the fullness of his light and glory, but the ability to see only comes with eyes adjusted to the light. This requires that we not just learn information *about* the Light, but that we ourselves experience transformation *by* the Light.

2 Corinthians 3:18 explains, "And we all, with unveiled face, beholding the glory of the Lord, are being transformed into the same image from one degree of glory to another. For this comes from the Lord who is the Spirit."

As we see, know, and understand the Father through the Son and by the power of the Holy Spirit, everything else falls into its right place. *This* is the secret wisdom about which Paul writes; however, it only occurs at the culmination of a process by which we seek to no longer conform to the world but be transformed by the renewing of our minds.

So why go to such great lengths to explain all this?

First, without the right lens, you will get lost. You won't understand how you are to live out your life in this world in light of eternity. What's more, you will struggle mightily in your fight against sin because you will continue to value what you are trying to resist. You will be resigned to "grinning and bearing" your way through a world of incessant temptations. If you allow the Holy Spirit to transform your worldview (and with it your desires), however, the way of Christian discipleship becomes clearer, and walking in that way becomes more natural, joyful, and truly freeing.

Second, I fear this is the current crisis within the church today. We are far more conformed to the image of the world than we are to the kingdom of heaven. We are spiritual regarding the message we profess, but we are worldly in the way we view our lives here on earth, and not just regarding sin. We have taught that "God gave us brains and the ability to use logic and reason so we could use them," but we have conflated worldly wisdom, logic, and reason with the wisdom of God.

I assure you, the wisdom of God is exceedingly logical and reasonable, but only if you understand eternity—only if you have been transformed by the renewing of your mind.

It is *quite* reasonable for the freedman returning to his former spot in the cave to no longer give concern to the shadows or the puppets. In the same way, it is *quite* reasonable for us to live by a new wisdom—one that is foolishness to the world—one that views comfort, self-preservation, reputation, selfish ambition, money, possessions, hardships, suffering, and even death radically different.

Where the church is built and governed by the wisdom of man, it will lack power, direction, and effectiveness; where the Christian has built his life on that same wisdom, so will his life be subject to the same end. He will be like the seed that has landed amongst the thorns: "This is the one who hears the word, but the cares of the world...choke the word, and it proves unfruitful" (Matthew 13:22).

Christian, I wonder if you have ever given consideration to how your worldview ought to be different than that of the rest of the world, not just in matters of sin, but in re-calibrating your basic understanding of wisdom—your entire measure for logic and reason? Has it changed what you value? Has it changed what you fear? What are the shadows with which you are still consuming yourself?

Brothers and sisters, do not value what the world values (Luke 16:15), and do not fear what the world fears (Isaiah 8:12), for we no longer see things the way the world does.

The Gospel changes *everything*.

We are merely moving shadows,

and all our busy rushing ends in nothing.

We heap up wealth,

not knowing who will spend it.

And so, Lord, where do I put my hope?

My only hope is in you.

-Psalm 39:6-7 (NLT)

CHAPTER 11 NOTES

[22]*National Treasure,* directed by Jon Turteltaub, (2004; Disney, (2005) dvd).

[23] Plato, *The Republic of Plato*, trans. F. M. Conford, (The Clarendon Press, Oxford, 1941), 222-226. By Permission of Oxford University Press.

[24] See Psalm 84:10.

[25] Isn't this what they did to our Jesus? He came to save the people from their sin, to set them free and lead them to the light, but they loved the darkness instead, so they killed him. His word says the same will be true of us if we follow him: "If the world hates you, know that it has hated me before it hated you. If you were of the world, the world would love you as its own; but because you are not of the world, but I chose you out of the world, therefore the world hates you. Remember the word that I said to you: 'A servant is not greater than his master.' If they persecuted me, they will also persecute you" (John 15:18-20).

[26] *The Republic of Plato, 225.*

[27] Ibid., 226.

[28] Ibid., 224-225.

XII.

RENEWING YOUR MIND

If we have surrendered to Christ, we have been united with him. We are tethered to him for the entirety of this journey, and he isn't letting go. He saves and he sanctifies. He sets free and he transforms. Jesus gets all the glory for our salvation and our sanctification, and it is only by fixing our eyes on him, the person of Jesus and not some list of legalisms, that our worldviews will be fully transformed as he intends.

But on this side of the divine curtain, what we do and how we respond to what he has called us to do matters; we have a role to play. So what does that look like regarding worldview? What is our role? How do we participate in transforming the lens through which we view all life?

Several years ago, I was caught in a cycle of recurring sin. The thing is, I genuinely wanted to stop the sin, but I felt powerless to do so. Like an addiction, despite my best intentions, when I was back in the moment, I would inevitably fail. Broken and ashamed, I fell before the Lord, pleading with him to take this sin from me or to give me strength from on high to be able to withstand the temptation as he had done on so many previous occasions. But God did not send an extra dosage of his sin-resisting power to me; instead, he was interested in growing me beyond my same cyclical patterns. He was interested in transforming me and the way I viewed the world, not just assisting me with strength to resist. It was time to grow up and move beyond "spiritual milk."

As I was praying, I distinctly felt as though God was pointing me to Romans 12:2: "Do not be conformed to this world, but be transformed by the renewal of your mind, that by testing you may discern what is the will of God, what is good and acceptable and perfect."

Yes! That was it. I needed God to transform my mind!

So I prayed, "Lord, I no longer want to continue in this cycle, battling this same recurring sin. Won't you transform my mind so that I no longer desire this temptation of the flesh?"

I was not prepared for the Lord's response. By the time I had finished the prayer, God had already responded, "How can I transform your mind when you continue to be entertained by the things of this world?"

I was cut to the core and fully convicted. You see, while I had not abandoned the routine of getting in the Word, or going to church and Bible study, I was spending a lot of time watching my favorite shows on Netflix, scrolling social media, and keeping up on the latest sports news. I realized all these things were subtly shaping the way I viewed the world.

The shows I was watching were not particularly inappropriate, vulgar, or profane, yet I knew they were influencing me. They were subtly shaping what I desired for my life—subtly suggesting the purpose of life is being "young and free," having loyal friendships, pursuing and finding romantic love, etc., subtly emphasizing the finite instead of the eternal. While it feels strange to admit it, if I watched enough of a particular show, I would find myself emulating the personalities and humor of the show's main characters. For all intents and purposes, I was being shaped by (conforming to) that which was entertaining me.

God created all of us to be shaped by that which we "wash" ourselves in. The imagery of being washed in the word comes from Ephesians 5 where Paul exhorts husbands to "wash" their wives in the word, so they can present their wives holy and blameless before the Lord. Each time we open up God's word to read; sit under good, Biblical teaching; or interact with anything or anyone that holds to a Biblical worldview, it begins to shape and transform us into Jesus' image, to see the world as he does.

The converse is also true, however. Every time we entertain ourselves with the things of this world, we are being washed in its ideologies, conformed slightly more into *its* image.

Psalm 1:1-3 reads: "Blessed is the man who walks not in the counsel of the wicked, nor stands in the way of sinners, nor sits in the seat of scoffers; but his delight is in the law of the Lord, and on his law he meditates day and night. He is like a tree planted by streams of water that yields its fruit in its season, and its leaf does not wither. In all that he does, he prospers."

We don't often think of the ways we entertain ourselves as "walking in the counsel of the wicked," but in many ways it is. We know the world is under the control of the Evil One (1 John 5:19), and 1 John 2:15-16 instructs: "Do not love the world or the things in the world. If anyone loves the world, the love of the Father is not in him. For all that is in the world—the desires of the flesh and the desires of the eyes and pride of life—is not from the Father but is from the world."

Do the things we are entertaining ourselves with teach us to treasure Jesus more—to value eternal things above all else? Or are the ideologies they are promoting built upon those of the world?

These are delicate waters, and I must tread carefully. I am not saying we can't ever watch our favorite shows, follow sports, or get on social media. That would be legalism *and* I would end up condemning myself, for the word says by whatever measure we judge others, we too will be judged (Matthew 7:2). So, in full transparency, I have not completely given these things up, and at times I give far too much of my time and attention to them.

But the word also says that while everything is permissible, not everything is beneficial (1 Corinthians 6:12, 10:23). Look again at Psalm 1:1-3: "Blessed is the man who...delight(s)...in the law of the Lord, and on his law he meditates day and night. He is like a tree planted by streams of water that yields its fruit in its season, and its leaf does not wither. In all that he does, he prospers."

It is God through the Spirit that transforms our minds—that reshapes our worldviews—but he does it largely by calling us to dig deeper into his Word, to wash ourselves in it, and to delight in it as we meditate on it day and night. But we can't do this, nor will we want to, if our leisure time is spent entertaining ourselves with the things of this world.

These forms of entertainment can be a blessing—aspects of God's common grace. Social media is an amazing way to stay connected with people, to network and communicate for business, and to mobilize as the church and spread the Gospel. Sports are a fun way to marvel at the Imago Dei (humans created in God's likeness), and what it can physically achieve. TV and movies can connect us with human emotions in a way that few things can; they can re-create history and tell wonderful stories. And sometimes, after a long hard day, it's nice to forget about the brokenness of the world for 22 minutes and enjoy a good laugh.

But good things can become idols. They can become distractions and hindrances from eternal things. For many of us, we allow these things to shape our worldviews and keep us in a prisoner-like mentality beyond what ought to be the case for the maturing Christian. For many of us, there is a large disconnect between what we believe and how we live because we don't want to step away from the comforts of the world to be transformed by the renewing of our minds by gazing upon the beauty of Christ as we "wash" ourselves in the Word.

We are either being "washed" in the word or "washed" in the world.

For some of us, the cost of giving up these forms of entertainment, even for just a few months, is too great. But my hope is that you would prayerfully consider your worldview, what's shaping it, and whether it is consistent with what you claim to believe.

Following the conviction I received that day as I prayed that God would deliver me from my cycle of sin, I was moved to fast for a couple of months from TV and non-work-related internet and social media. I spent the time immersing myself in the word and learning to be still. It was painful; I felt like an addict going through withdrawal. I didn't know how to deal with silence and an absence of constant mental and visual stimulation. I hadn't realized how dependent upon these things I had become to keep myself from being bored. Checking social media and browsing the Internet on my phone had become a compulsive habit.

In 1 Kings 19:11-12, God tells Elijah to go out and stand on the mount in order to hear a word from the Lord. It says a great wind passed by, but the Lord wasn't in the wind. Then it says there was an earthquake, but the Lord was not in the earthquake. This was followed by a fire, but he wasn't in the fire either. Finally, following the fire, the Lord spoke in a whisper.

Undoubtedly, the Lord can speak to us at any time and in any way he wants. Nonetheless, he often chooses to whisper, so that we can only hear him if we are still—if we turn off the distractions, get away from the noise, and earnestly and intentionally seek him.

I realized that even my time in the word had been affected by the busyness of my mind. It was always cluttered with the excess of information and stimulation with which I constantly flooded it. This time of fasting helped detox my mind, which enabled my time in the word to be more fruitful. Spiritually, it was one of the most beneficial seasons of my life. I grew exponentially in intimacy with the Lord, and he was faithful to transform my mind and my worldview more into his Image.

I gradually returned to these forms of media/entertainment, and for a while I was able to keep them in check; however, I have recently found myself increasingly attached to them. "Like a dog returning to its vomit," I have returned to my former folly (Proverbs 26:11), even after knowing what was to be gained by staying away. Once again, I feel the Lord calling me to a season of fasting—of unbridled pursuit of him and his Word.

We are called to be transformed by the renewing of our minds. Why? So we can discern the good, acceptable, and perfect will of God. Only if we're looking through the right lens will we be able to discern the way to get to and fully take hold of the treasure: Jesus Himself. It might hurt to surrender some of the things that are subtly shaping us. But, then again, it will always hurt to go from being a prisoner to being free, to go from living in the darkness to living in the light. But it is always worth it.

As we begin to understand this, it changes our entire relationship to pain and suffering. In fact, that is exactly what we'll be discussing in the next chapter.

XIII.

TREASURING PAIN

Treasuring pain—that is an unusual concept, isn't it? How could you treasure pain? Yet, this seems to be a prevailing sentiment throughout Scripture and the history of Christianity. Charles Spurgeon eloquently put it, "I have learned to kiss the wave that slams me into the Rock of Ages."

Consider It Pure Joy

When he was 14 years old, Arnold Schwarzenegger made a decision: he was going to be the greatest bodybuilder the sport had ever seen. But he knew if he was going to accomplish this, he was going to have to work for it; it wasn't going to be handed to him. He began training for hours every day—sometimes as much as 6-8 hours per day.

As most of you know, the only way to build muscle is to break it down. This means you have to perform exercises with enough of a load that it literally tears the muscle fibers. Then, with proper rest and nutrition, your body repairs the muscle, leaving it bigger and stronger. In order for substantial change to occur, you must continually increase the amount of work you are asking the muscles to do, overloading them to the point of failure and continually creating tears in the fibers. And guess what? It hurts!

Wouldn't it be great if there was a way to shortcut the pain? Wouldn't it be great if there was an easier, more comfortable way? I think we can all agree we would like to be more fit, *and* we would like it if we could get that way without the pain. Unfortunately, there is no other way. So we come to a crossroad, and we are forced to count the cost—to conduct a cost-benefit analysis. The question we're faced with is this: "Is it worth it?" Do we value the change that will occur enough to endure, even self-inflict, the pain necessary to achieve the change?

For Arnold, the answer was a resounding "yes." He so valued the change, he so treasured in his heart the end result, that it actually changed the way he viewed pain. In one of his most telling quotes, he says, "Pain makes me grow. Growth is what I want. So for me, pain is pleasure." He actually started to desire the pain because he knew it was producing in him that which he desired most! For Arnold, the pain of that extra rep, and that extra set, was pure joy! It was bringing him one step closer to his destination.

It would seem as though God wired Christian growth in much the same way he did muscular growth. James 1:2-4 reads, "Count it all joy, my brothers, when you meet trials of various kinds, for you know that the testing of your faith produces steadfastness. And let steadfastness have its full effect, that you may be perfect and complete, lacking in nothing." Similarly, Romans 5:3-5 contends, "We rejoice in our sufferings, knowing that suffering produces endurance, and endurance produces character, and character produces hope, and hope does not put us to shame, because God's love has been poured into our hearts through the Holy Spirit who has been given to us." Here,

Paul and James are saying the same thing: we can rejoice in our trials because our trials are producing spiritual maturity.

But spiritual maturity is not an end in itself; we don't desire maturity just to be more mature. Rather, it is by growing in maturity that as Christians we take hold more fully of Jesus. Christian maturity, by definition, means we know Jesus more intimately and trust him more fully.

Remember the prisoner from the cave?

As the rescuer frees the prisoner from his chains and places his arm around his shoulders to assist him in climbing the steep ascent to the cave entrance, can you imagine the pain he (the prisoner) would feel? If I sit still for more than a few hours at a time, my muscles start to tighten up and my joints ache. How much more for someone who has never before stood or walked?

The ascent would be nearly impossible. Even with the man who set him free bearing most of the load, it is likely the pain would be excruciating. His lungs would burn. He would stumble and fall—scraping his knees, piercing his skin, and unleashing a steady flow of fresh blood from his wounds. With each step closer to the entrance of the cave, the light would become more blinding. Finally, as he is thrust onto the soft grass on the outside of the cave, the light would be overwhelming. Even with his eyes closed, the thin layer of protection his eyelids provided would do little to alleviate the pain of the bright sun to eyes that had only known darkness.

Nonetheless, as he is set free from his chains and begins the ascent, with each step he would grow in his understanding of the truth. He would see behind him for the first time. He would observe the fire that had cast the light on the wall in front of him. He would glimpse the puppets carved by wood and stone. He would make out his captors—men who looked just like him, but who were not bound by the same chains he had been. He would begin to understand he was a prisoner, and there was more to life than what he had known. The images on the cave wall were not real at all; they were merely shadows manipulated to create an illusion—a false reality. He would realize his whole life had been a lie. Everything he thought had mattered didn't. He would be enlightened in the truest sense of the word.

It would be reasonable for the prisoner from the cave to be apprehensive at first, or even resistant to the man setting him free, because of the pain he was causing. But with each step and the truth it revealed, a trust would begin to form. For he would see that, despite the pain, what was happening was producing a far better end than staying in his chains. While each step was painful, even more so, it was profitable. He knew his rescuer understood something he didn't. By the time the man's eyes adjusted to the beauty of being free in the light, there would be not a shadow of a doubt that the pain was worth it and that his rescuer was good—exceedingly good—worthy of all trust.

So as he tethers himself to his savior, desiring to learn all he can about this new reality, how do you suppose he will respond the next time the man leads him into a painful situation? Will he remember the way in which the pain from the cave resulted in exceeding beauty and freedom? Will he trust his savior as he stands on the precipice of a dark valley or a steep ascent to a mountain top? Will he trust that the pain will be worth reaching the destination and that a greater amount of beauty and freedom is waiting on the other side?

The pain was not for nothing; it had purpose, and the man who set him free understood that. He was willing to force him into this pain because it was the necessary path to freedom.

So it is with us. Every painful event in our lives is an opportunity. It is the Lord, in his grace, carefully and lovingly directing us to a greater understanding of truth, to greater freedom, and to a greater trust in the One who set us free—Jesus Christ.

We have two options: we can remain in our chains, or we can experience the pain of learning to walk, learning to climb, and moving from the darkness into the light. There is no third option; the prisoner cannot ascend out of the cave in a way that isn't painful. His ascent necessitates pain, as does our ascent to Christian maturity.

Psalm 84:5-6 (NIV) reads, "Blessed are those whose strength is in you, whose hearts are set on pilgrimage. As they pass through the Valley of Baka, they make it a place of springs; the autumn rains also cover it with pools."

For many pilgrims, in order to get to the temple on Mount Zion, they would have to pass through the Valley of Baka (also known as the Valley of Weeping or Mourning). It would undoubtedly be the most treacherous part of the journey. The extreme heat and low annual rainfall would make the conditions nearly unbearable and the way nearly impassable.[29] Weary travelers would be parched, famished, and sun-scorched; yet, there was no other way to get to the mount. There was no way around it; if you wanted to get to the temple—to the courts of the Lord—then you had to journey through the valley. But the Psalmist says the one who has set his heart on pilgrimage makes it a "place of springs"—a place of joy. This is because the one who treasures the Lord above all else says, "Traveling through the valley leads me to the Lord; the Lord is what I want, so for me, the valley is a place of joy."

Arnold counted as joy the pain of lifting weights because his heart treasured the result more than it did comfort. The Psalmist counted as joy the most deadly and dangerous part of the pilgrimage to the temple because he treasured the destination more than his comfort. The question we then have to ask is this: do we treasure Jesus more than we treasure comfort and avoiding pain? Do we desire to grow in our relationship with Jesus enough to embrace the pain necessary to get there, even self-inflicting it at times, practicing the disciplines of the Christian faith (i.e., prayer, scripture reading, fasting, solitude, etc.)?

The apostle Paul did.

When I hear Arnold's quote, I can't help but think of the Apostle Paul's words in Philippians: "For to me to live is Christ, and to die is gain" (Philippians 1:21). He is saying his worldview has been so radically transformed by the Gospel that it has fundamentally changed how he lives his life, what he treasures, and even how he views death. He is essentially saying, "Jesus is what I want. Death brings me closer to him; therefore, for me, to die is gain." It is a verse that encapsulates the way Paul lived his life, and we see time and time again specific examples of Paul living it out.

Acts 21 is one of these examples. Here, Paul is trying to make his way to Jerusalem because of a prompting by the Holy Spirit to go and preach the good news there. He desperately wants to make it there by Pentecost. He and the men he is with have recently set sail from Macedonia to Greece to Syria and now have arrived in Caesarea, which is the last stop before they arrive in Jerusalem. They have spent several days there with some Christian brothers, and that's where we'll pick up.

Acts 21:10-11 reads, "While we were staying for many days, a prophet named Agabus came down from Judea. And coming to us, he took Paul's belt and bound his own feet and hands and said, "Thus says the Holy Spirit, 'This is how the Jews at Jerusalem will bind the man who owns this belt and deliver him into the hands of the Gentiles.'"

Paul is going to Jerusalem because the Holy Spirit has told him to, but then the Holy Spirit sends a prophet to Paul, telling him if he goes to Jerusalem he's going to suffer. He seems to be getting mixed messages, and this isn't the first time it has happened; in fact, it keeps happening. A chapter earlier, Paul explains, "And now, behold, I am going to Jerusalem, constrained by the Spirit, not knowing what will happen to me there, except that the Holy Spirit testifies to me in every city that imprisonment and afflictions await me" (Acts 20:22-23).

And then verse 4 of chapter 21 says, "Through the Spirit they [the disciples] were telling Paul not to go on to Jerusalem."

But Paul isn't getting mixed messages. For Paul, it is completely reasonable that God would be telling him not only that prison and hardships await him in Jerusalem, but also that he wants him to go there. Paul already knows it, but it seems as if God wants to make sure everyone around him also knows that Paul is going to suffer if he goes to Jerusalem and wants to make it equally clear that he is still calling Paul to go there.

We see from the text that when the people around Paul hear he is going to suffer, they automatically assume he shouldn't go. In their minds, suffering is bad. That seems like a pretty legitimate thought pattern, right? I think it's a thought to which most of us can relate. We might even be getting a little uncomfortable right now thinking about how a loving God could be asking Paul to walk directly into imminent suffering, and we're even more uncomfortable with the thought that God could be asking us to do the same. That's what's happening in this passage, however. God is making it clear that he is calling Paul to choose suffering.

All the people in Paul's life are trying to convince him not to go to Jerusalem, but Paul doesn't listen because he doesn't think the way they do. He's not worried about suffering; it doesn't concern him. More importantly, it doesn't control him. Comfort and security do not dictate what Paul does. This is because Paul has learned to see things as God does—through his lens.

In verse 13, Paul asks, "What are you doing, weeping and breaking my heart? For I am ready not only to be imprisoned but even to die in Jerusalem for the name of the Lord Jesus."

Paul is not begrudgingly following Jesus and going into Jerusalem where prison and hardship await; he does so gladly. Many years prior, on the road to Damascus, Paul encountered King Jesus (Acts 9),

One worthy of reorienting his entire life. He chose then to follow Jesus, and since then, through countless trials and hardships, he has come to believe, in the very core of his being, that "to live is Christ and to die is gain." It is not hyperbole to him to say it is pure joy when he faces trials of many kinds. This is because Paul knows that trials, pain, suffering, and even death will all give him more of what he treasures most: Christ himself.

What we treasure in our heart changes how we view the world; it determines how we view pain, suffering, and even death. When we treasure Jesus above all else, we too learn to "kiss the wave that slams us into the Rock of Ages."

It will always hurt to go from being a prisoner to being free—from living in the darkness to living in the light. It will always hurt to surrender our attachments and repent of our idols. It will always hurt to be purged of our addictions and suffer through withdrawals, and it will always hurt to beat (discipline) our body and make it our slave (1 Corinthians 9:27). But it is always worth it because it leads us to that which we desire most—more of Jesus.

This doesn't mean that all suffering is the same, or that life doesn't ever rock us. It certainly doesn't mean that certain tragedies, illnesses, and losses aren't heartbreaking travesties that deserve to be deeply grieved. Life has the ability to be indescribably painful. The evil that occurs in this world on a daily basis is a constant reminder that things are not as they should be—as God created them to be. The Devil is still at work, and sin is still pervasive—infecting and affecting everything it touches. Perhaps these evils have even touched your life in a very personal way; perhaps unspeakable tragedy has come upon you or those closest to you.

Allowing the Gospel to transform the way you view pain doesn't mean you don't feel the depths of that pain. Rather, it means that as we stand on the precipice of a dark valley or a steep ascent, we can trust fully in the One to whom we are tethered. If he is leading us, no amount of pain will be wasted. The worst that life can throw at us will only serve to help us know Jesus more, and in this we can find joy.

Act 21:14-15 reads: "And since he would not be persuaded, we ceased and said, 'Let the will of the Lord be done.' After these days we got ready and went up to Jerusalem."

Paul counted the cost and he went. Paul eventually would die a martyr's death, but we can see that he first lived a martyr's life. In Acts 20:24 he says, "But I do not account my life of any value nor as precious to myself, if only I may finish my course and the ministry that I received from the Lord Jesus, to testify to the Gospel of the grace of God."

He had encountered something so magnificently beautiful and life-changing that, prison or free, suffering or not, living or dead, it made no difference to Paul as long as he had Jesus. Can we say the same?

One of the most important ways in which the Gospel reshapes our ideologies is regarding our perspective on pain. This is essential because if we continue to view pain and discomfort in the same way, we will never make the proverbial ascent out of the "cave." We will stagnate in our discipleship, unwilling to go where Jesus is trying to lead us.

We live in a "have your cake and eat it too" world. We want to be fit, but we don't want to pay the cost. We don't want to endure the pain of the extra reps and denial of indulgences it will take to get there. We quite literally want to eat our cake too.

Spiritually, we want to experience more of God, but we don't want it to cost anything. We don't want to have to give up anything, to have to deny ourselves comfort and pleasure, and we certainly don't want to have to experience pain. But there is no other way.

Christian, what do you treasure most?

CHAPTER 13 NOTES

[29] While there is much ambiguity as to the exact location of this valley, most scholars agree it would be an extremely dry, barren, and gloomy valley that was necessary to pass through in order to reach the temple. It would be particularly treacherous during hot seasons.

PART IV:
THE ENEMIES OF
FAITH

Following Jesus takes faith because it often asks of us things that are counter to our natural dispositions. It often asks us to jump in spite of very real and reasonable fear. Following Jesus is often counter to every inclination we have; it is hard, messy, and dangerous. With that comes the constant temptation to act apart from the faith that we claim.

We have no shortages of enemies of our faith. Specifically, the Bible talks about the Devil and our own sinful nature being in opposition to walking out our faith. These enemies attack us in the form of fear, self-preservation, selfish gain, self-autonomy, and others.

In this section, we will take a deeper look at Satan, his deviant schemes to impede upon our faith, and the ways in which God has equipped us to protect against his attacks. We will also look at some of the specific ways we are tempted by our own desires to act in contradiction to our faith and what it looks like to follow Jesus in these situations instead of succumbing to our sin.

The "enemies" covered are not exhaustive, but my prayer is that as you read and reflect, you would be able to identify these and other similar inhibitors of faith in your own life.

XIV.

Spiritual Warfare

Beneath the streets of Canterbury, England, on a dirty wall in a dimly lit corridor of the city's vast subway, a poem recently appeared. It reads:

> "Today they killed the monster,
>   So the war should end now,
> But I know it will not,
>   For there was no monster,
> The real monster made the monster up,
>   Stop the monster."
>   –A poem by The Kid[30]

What the poem seems to suggest is that we while we tend to fixate on a flesh-and-blood enemy, thinking a person or group of people to be the root of our problems, there is in fact a far more sinister opponent at work against humanity. We tend to fixate on the major threats of this world: Hitler, Stalin, Bin-Laden, Al-Qaeda, ISIS, North

Korea, or Kim Jung-Un. Perhaps we view the "monster" on a more domestic scale: Trump or Obama, the Republicans or the Democrats. But what the author of this poem is suggesting is that while many of these men have done very evil things, they are not, in fact, the real enemy; they are merely a distraction. They are decoys to keep us from taking up arms against the real enemy—the true Monster behind the "monster."

As Christians, we are at war. We have an enemy that seeks to devour and destroy us, our faith, and everything we hold most dear to us. And, like the poem, this enemy is not a flesh-and-blood opponent. It is not our boss, parent, president, neighbor, ex, spouse, or any other person who has deeply wounded us. It is not a person or group of people, foreign or domestic. It is not white people, black people, or Mexicans. In fact, our enemy is not a person at all; these things are but decoys.

Paul explains, "For we do not wrestle against flesh and blood, but against the rulers, against the authorities, against the cosmic powers over this present darkness, against the spiritual forces of evil in the heavenly places" (Ephesians 6:12). Our real enemy is none other than Satan himself (and his army of demons), and he's out for blood. Peter warns, "Be sober-minded; be watchful. Your adversary the devil prowls around like a roaring lion, seeking someone to devour" (1 Peter 5:8).

If we remain fixated on a material problem as our enemy, we will be distracted from the battle that is being waged for our faith and for our soul. In 2 Corinthians 2:11 (NIV), Paul urges the church in Corinth to live out the implications of their faith by extending forgiveness to an offender, "in order that Satan might not outwit us. For we are not unaware of his schemes." But can we say the same? Are we aware of the devil's schemes? Do we know how to protect against them, or are we being outwitted by him?

In his article, "The Generous Gambler," Charles Baudelaire wisely surmises, "My dear brethren, do not ever forget...that the loveliest trick of the Devil is to persuade you that he does not exist!"[31] C.S. Lewis expands upon this idea in his book *The Screwtape Letters* in which a demon mentors his nephew through a series of letters on how to disarm, discourage, and disrupt a person's belief and deliver him successfully into hell. In response to the younger's inquiry about whether to make his presence known, the older demon replies:

> I do not think you will have much difficulty in keeping the patient in the dark. The fact that "devils" are predominantly comic figures in the modern imagination will help you. If any faint suspicion of your existence begins to arise in his mind, suggest to him a picture of something in red tights, and persuade him that since he cannot believe in that (it is an old textbook method of confusing them) he therefore cannot believe in you.[32]

In the preface to this work, Lewis explains, "There are two equal and opposite errors into which our race can fall about the devils. One is to disbelieve in their existence. The other is to believe, and to feel an excessive and unhealthy interest in them."[33] For most of us, we struggle with the former. We either don't believe in Satan and demons, or we do, but we don't give much thought to them or the idea that we are at war.

The thing is, you can't read the Bible and claim to believe what it says without accepting that an enemy exists and that he is trying to destroy you. Jesus casts out demons (Matthew 8:28-34), teaches about Satan (John 8:44), and even encounters him in Matthew 4 when he is tempted in the desert. What's more, Peter, Paul, and John all give warnings about Satan and spiritual warfare in their letters to the early church. Archibald Brown contends, "The existence of the devil is so clearly taught in the Bible that to doubt it is to doubt the Bible itself."[34]

Most of the time, however, spiritual warfare will not look anything like the Hollywood portrayal. Instead, it will come in the form of subtle and crafty attempts to undermine and erode our faith in Jesus and his word.

If faith is the right response to that which we claim to believe, the enemy's goal is to hinder that right response. Satan's primary objective is to keep us from putting our faith in Jesus. If this fails and we become a regenerate believer, his objective becomes to inhibit our spiritual growth and maturity by keeping our faith riddled with doubt. He wants to hinder us from experiencing the transformative effects of our conversion and to inflict as much hurt and pain in us and through us (as we wound other people around us) as a result of our immaturity as he possibly can. In doing so, he seeks to make our witness to the surrounding world not only ineffective but counterproductive. In short, Satan's aim is to destroy our faith, rendering it useless.

We are at war, and Satan is a more-than-formidable foe; he is smarter, more cunning, and more powerful than we are. We stand little chance in the battle if we attempt to fight him on our own. Luckily, as Christians, we don't have to fight the battle on our own.

1 John 4:4 encourages, "Little children, you are from God and have overcome them [evil spirits], for he who is in you is greater than he who is in the world." 1 John 5:4-5 adds, "For everyone who has been born of God overcomes the world. And this is the victory that has overcome the world—our faith. Who is it that overcomes the world except the one who believes that Jesus is the Son of God?"

Satan is no match for the power of God. There is only one holy, transcendent, sovereign Creator. Lucifer was a creation of God; he is not his equal. In Matthew 8:28-31, we see demons begging Jesus not to torture them before the appointed time. They do not even consider taking him on!

The war has already been won. On the cross, Jesus defeated Satan, overcoming sin and death. But even though this is true, until Jesus returns and that victory is enforced, we will continue to be bombarded by an Enemy who wants to destroy us and our faith. Thankfully, we have been given authority in Christ over the powers of the Enemy, armor to protect us, and weapons with which to fight.

Because of the cross, we have been given authority both to bear Jesus' name and to exercise the power of that name. James 4:7 says, "Submit yourselves therefore to God. Resist the devil, and he will flee from you." In Luke 10:18-19 (NIV) Jesus says, "I saw Satan fall like lightning from heaven. I have given you authority to trample on snakes and scorpions and to overcome the power of the enemy. Nothing will harm you."

We have everything we need in Christ Jesus to fight off the enemy until he (Jesus) returns. In Ephesians 6, following Paul's teaching that our battle is not against flesh and blood, he instructs:

> Therefore take up the whole armor of God, that you may be able to withstand in the evil day, and having done all, to stand firm. Stand therefore, having fastened on the belt of truth, and having put on the breastplate of righteousness, and, as shoes for your feet, having put on the readiness given by the gospel of peace. In all circumstances take up the shield of faith, with which you can extinguish all the flaming darts of the evil one; and take the helmet of salvation, and the sword of the Spirit, which is the word of God, praying at all times in the Spirit, with all prayer and supplication. To that end, keep alert with all perseverance, making supplication for all the saints, (Ephesians 6:13-18).

We have been provided with armor to protect us from the Enemy. In the passage I have just cited, Paul uses the metaphor of a Roman soldier to explain this "armor" clearly. In Paul's day, a soldier's armor, because of the intensity of battle, would eventually get worn down and be useless. It would have to be constantly maintained, repaired, or replaced because going into battle with armor at less than 100% could be a fatal mistake.

So it is with us. We must learn to actively and continuously put on the protection God has provided for us. Chip Ingram explains, "This is a lifestyle, not a checklist. These pieces of protection aren't things that we can mechanically pray onto ourselves each morning in a step-by-step routine. It is a visual aid to help us understand how to live out a relationship with the Father in the power of the Holy Spirit...the product of weeks, months, and years of practice and cultivation."[35]

As we look closer at this armor, notice how Paul maintains the tension of grace (Belt of Truth, Helmet of Salvation, Feet Fitted with the Readiness of the Gospel) and obedience (Breastplate of Righteousness and Shield of Faith). Neglecting to put on any of these pieces will make us vulnerable to Satan's attacks.

The Belt of Truth

If you or I don't put on a belt, we might have trouble keeping our pants up. For a soldier in Paul's day, the consequences would be much greater. The belt was the part of the armor that held everything together. The soldier's weapon, his rations, his tunic—everything connected into the belt. Without it, the rest of his armor was useless. The same is true for the Christian without truth.

In John 14:6, Jesus claims that he *is* the Truth, and in 18:37 he proclaims that he came to bear witness to the truth. Part of this truth is that he came to save sinners, not the righteous (Luke 5:32, 1 Timothy 1:15). Thus, 1 John 1:8 calls us to live in transparency (to be truthful) regarding our sin: "If we claim to be without sin, we deceive ourselves and the truth is not in us. If we confess our sins, he is faithful and just and will forgive us our sins and purify us from all unrighteousness. If we claim we have not sinned, we make him out to be a liar and his word has no place in our lives."

Christian, are you trusting in the truth of who Jesus is, and are you allowing this truth to empower you to walk in transparency regarding sin in your life?

Our protection from the Enemy hinges upon our own willingness and ability to be truthful and transparent regarding our sin and brokenness, and to hold tightly to the truths about who Jesus is as revealed in the Bible. Chip Ingram explains, "We are to train our minds to see God, ourselves, and others through the clear lens of what he says is true.... [This means] we're honest with God, honest with ourselves, and honest with others."[36]

Honesty holds it all together.

The Breastplate of Righteousness

A soldier's breastplate helped protect his most vital organs—most importantly, his heart.

Biologically speaking, the heart is the organ that pumps the blood that gives life throughout our bodies. If it stops working—getting damaged in too great of a way, we die. When the Bible talks about the heart, it is not referring to the organ, but rather to the innermost place within us out of which our feelings, thoughts, and actions flow. It is also the place out of which our spiritual lifeblood flows. If we allow our "heart" to absorb too much damage, our very faith is in jeopardy. This is why Proverbs 4:23 urges, "Keep your heart with all vigilance, for from it flow the springs of life."

Paul is contending that righteousness serves as a way to protect one's heart from the Enemy's attacks. Although we have an objective righteousness that has been credited to us because of the Great Exchange of the Gospel, what Paul is referring to is subjective righteousness: are we living according to God's word?

Sin creates a chink in the breastplate of righteousness: it hardens our hearts, quenches the Spirit, embitters us toward God, and makes us (and our faith) susceptible to the Enemy's attacks. Christian, are you willfully engaging in sin?

"Do not give the devil a foothold!" (Ephesians 4:27, NIV)

Feet Fitted with the Readiness of the Gospel

A soldier's sandals were designed specifically to maximize his footing to withstand a charge from the enemy. In order for this to be effective, the soldier's footing would have to be deeply anchored to the ground. Thus, the sandals were often fitted with spikes on the sole to create a firmer grip.

With the right footwear, a first-century soldier could become an immovable force. So it is with us—the Gospel is our foundation and our root, and it empowers us to stand steadfast regardless of the Enemy's onslaughts, regardless of whatever life throws at us. The Gospel assures us of our salvation, God's love for us, and our right standing before him, as he has given us the right to become Children of God. For the Christian, there is no condemnation in Christ Jesus (Romans 8:1).

There is hardly a better picture of this than the prophecy in Zechariah 3:1-5 (NIV):

> Then he showed me Joshua the high priest standing before the angel of the Lord, and Satan standing at his right side to accuse him. The Lord said to Satan, "The Lord rebuke you, Satan! The Lord, who has chosen Jerusalem, rebuke you! Is not this man a burning stick snatched from the fire?"
>
> Now Joshua was dressed in filthy clothes as he stood before the angel. The angel said to those who were standing before him, "Take off his filthy clothes."
>
> Then he said to Joshua, "See, I have taken away your sin, and I will put fine garments on you."

Then I said, "Put a clean turban on his head." So they put a clean turban on his head and clothed him, while the angel of the Lord stood by.

Joshua was filthy; there was no denying it, hiding it, nor getting around it. Yet, as Satan stood by to point out Joshua's filth, it was Satan who was rebuked. As for Joshua, the Lord took away his filthy garments and replaced them with fine ones; he took away his sin and clothed him with righteousness. What more is there for Satan to say?

So it is with us as we are rooted in the Gospel: the devil has no foothold; he has no angle against us. Yes, he might be right as he exposes our filth, but our love and acceptance in Christ are not based on our cleanliness. Quite the contrary, it is because of our filth that Christ died in our stead; therefore, although the Enemy tries to accuse us, he is not revealing anything that God did not already know when he sent his Son to die for us. As Martin Luther declares, "So when the devil throws your sins in your face and declares that you deserve death and hell, tell him this: 'I admit that I deserve death and hell, what of it? For I know One who suffered and made satisfaction on my behalf. His name is Jesus Christ, Son of God, and where He is there I shall be also!'"[37]

In this we have victory. Through Christ, we find the firm footing that makes us immovable in an attack from the Enemy. The Gospel makes impotent the accusations of Satan.

Christian, are you daily preaching the Gospel to yourself?

The Shield of Faith, With Which You Can Extinguish All the Flaming Darts of the Evil One

It was not uncommon for an opposing army to quite literally shoot flaming arrows, hoping to inflict as much damage on their foe, their chariots, and their camp as possible. Thus, a good shield was constructed to both absorb and extinguish the flaming weapons.

Paul is telling us that our faith is similar.

He knows that in this life we will be bombarded with temptations and tribulations; Jesus promised as much (James 1:4; John 16:33). When these temptations and tribulations come, we can expect a full onslaught of accusations and perversions of the truth from the Enemy. His attacks will not only have the ability to pierce, but to start a fire that threatens to burn up our trust and belief in Jesus.

Doubt and unbelief are the flaming arrows of the Evil One. The Enemy will do everything he can to get us to doubt the promises of God, and his love, goodness, wisdom, and sovereignty. Isn't this the Serpent's tactic in the Garden, as he repeatedly asks, "Did God really say...?"

We mustn't let doubt win. James 1:6-7 explains, "The one who doubts is like a wave of the sea that is driven and tossed by the wind. For that person must not suppose that he will receive anything from the Lord; he is a double-minded man, unstable in all his ways."

What is the solution? Paul tells us to arm ourselves with faith!

Hebrews 11:1 says, "Faith is the assurance of things hoped for, the conviction of things not seen." This means when we come to the valley, the difficult terrain, and the most arduous parts of the journey, we do not turn back; we do not lose hope. Rather, we press on because we believe in the promises of God.

Faith is an action built on a truth; it is a manifestation of a professed belief. Because of the Gospel and the truths in Scripture concerning God's character, we can trust that he is working all things together for the (ultimate) good of those who love him (Romans 8:28). We can live in light of this truth.

This is faith, and it extinguishes even the Enemy's most perilous attacks.

The Helmet of Salvation

If a soldier is going to war, there isn't much that is more important to protect than his head, for obvious reasons. While he might recover from a flesh wound, a sword, an arrow, or a good ol' fashioned bludgeoning to the head would have dire and permanent consequences. Even if he survived, it would most likely cost him the ability to function normally.

This is because the mind is crucial to our functionality. If our minds get damaged physically, the rest of us can't function properly. The same is true spiritually.

There is a battle for our minds that is waging. How we think, our worldviews, and what we believe, radically affects the way we live our lives, and Satan wants nothing more than to infiltrate our minds and start planting false truths. But God has called and equipped us to put on a helmet of protection to keep the enemy out. We do this by the renewing and the transforming of our minds (as we have already discussed) by the Spirit as we "wash" ourselves in the Word.

With every attack against truth that the Enemy levies against us, we have the Helmet of Salvation to enable us to take those thoughts captive, destroy enemy strongholds, and emerge victoriously from the onslaught.

2 Corinthians 10:3-5 reads, "For though we walk in the flesh, we are not waging war according to the flesh. For the weapons of our warfare are not of the flesh but have divine power to destroy strongholds. We destroy arguments and every lofty opinion raised against the knowledge of God, and take every thought captive to obey Christ."

Christian, take seriously the battle that is going on for your mind.

The Sword of the Spirit, Which is the Word of God

God has equipped us not only with armor to protect us from the enemy's attacks, but with a weapon to fight back and secure victory: the Sword of the Spirit, which is the word of God.

When we see this verse through the lens of our own bias, we might be tempted to focus on one half. We might say, "See! Our greatest weapon is the Holy Spirit!" or "Ah-ha! I told you that the Bible was our most important asset." Truth be told, however, what we see here (once again) is the divinely held tension of walking in both Spirit and in Truth.

Chip Ingram explains:

> Most times in New Testament Greek, *word* is a translation of *logos*. Not here. In this case, it's a translation of *rhema*—the specific spoken word given to us by the Spirit of God to do close, hand-to-hand combat with the lies and deceptions of the enemy. God applies his word (*rhema*) by making the word (*logos*) alive and active in our specific situations.... The difference between the *logos* and the *rhema* is the difference between a stockpile of weapons and a sword in a highly skilled hand. One is the invaluable arsenal; the other is a specific, well-timed deployment. The *rhema* is the sword of the Spirit.[38]

In Matthew 4:3-11, Jesus is led by the Spirit out to the desert to fast for forty days. As the forty days draw to a close, Satan arrives on the scene with the intent to tempt Jesus away from God's will. But with each temptation that Satan presents, Jesus responds with "It is written..." followed by a Scripture that directly refutes the temptation Satan has levied against him. As a result, Jesus is able to withstand all three temptations. In John 12:49, we learn that Jesus does not speak on his own, but only what he hears from the Father. Similarly, through the Spirit, we have Jesus and the Father with us to bring Scriptures we have previously learned to mind in the heat of battle.

We must be filled with the Spirit, adept to hearing his voice, and rooted firmly in knowledge of the written Word. This is a matter of life and death.

Christian, are you actively seeking to grow in both Spirit and Truth—praying for the Spirit and studying the Word?

The Final Piece

Finally, pray! Paul concludes the "armor passage" with this command: "[Pray] at all times in the Spirit, with all prayer and supplication. To that end, keep alert with all perseverance, making supplication for all the saints," (Ephesians 6:18). Without prayer, we are going into battle alone. Thus, prayer is perhaps our greatest and most powerful weapon.

* * * * *

Satan is not the cause of our sin. He is not the reason we doubt, or the reason there is a disconnect between what we claim to believe and how we live our lives. The Bible makes clear that we are each tempted "when [we] are dragged away by [our] own evil desire and enticed. Then, after desire has conceived, it gives birth to sin; and sin, when it is full-grown, gives birth to death" (James 1:14-15, NIV). In fact, the remaining chapters in this section will focus on "enemies" that arise from our flesh.

In Satan, however, we do have a very real and dangerous adversary that is seeking to destroy us and our faith—exposing and exploiting every weakness, wound, temptation, and sin within us.

We are at war, and the only way we will survive—the only way Satan doesn't succeed in disrupting and disarming our faith—is for us to equip, train, and surrender. We must continually equip ourselves with the Armor of God. We must train ourselves to know our armor and be proficient in it. Finally, above all else, we must surrender to the One in whom real power rests: victory comes in the name of Jesus.

> *"Be sober-minded; be watchful.*
> *Your adversary the devil*
> *prowls around like a roaring lion,*
> *seeking someone to devour."*
> *-1 Peter 5:8*

CHAPTER 14 NOTES

30 Source unknown.

31 Charles Baudelaire. The Generous Gambler. 1864. (Public Domain).

32 THE SCREWTAPE LETTERS by C.S. LEWIS copyright © C.S. Lewis Pte. Ltd. 1942. Extracts reprinted by permission. (HarperCollins, New York, 2001), 32.

33 THE SCREWTAPE LETTERS by C.S. LEWIS, IX (Preface).

34 Original source unknown.

35 Chip Ingram, *The Invisible War*, (Baker Books, Grand Rapids, 2006), 75. Used by permission.

36 Ibid., 83.

37 Martin Luther, Letters of Spiritual Counsel, trans. and ed. Theodore G. Tappert, (Vancouver, British Columbia: Regent College, 2003), 86–87. Used by permission.

38 Ingram, *The Invisible War*,140.

XV.

FIGHTING PHOBOS

In the year 480 B.C., King Xerxes and an army of nearly two million Persian soldiers sought to invade and enslave all of Greece. This, however, required the army to pass by foot through a narrow pass between ocean and mountains. The opening was so narrow that the sheer numbers of the Persian army would be at least partially neutralized in battle. As the Persians approached this pass, known as the Gates of Fire, they found 300 hand-selected Spartan warriors armed for battle and waiting for them.

These 300 men valiantly fought back the relentless encroachment of the massive Persian army for seven days, killing nearly 20,000 of the opposition's best soldiers. By the end of the seventh day, all 300 of the Spartan warriors had given their lives to the battle, but their heroic stand for those seven days provided ample time (as well as inspiration) for the Greeks to assemble the necessary arms to defeat the Persians and ensure their ongoing freedom. The Spartans and their warrior culture would go down in infamy.

In the book *Gates of Fire*, a historical fiction novel about this epic battle, the author Steven Pressfield provides insight into the warrior culture of the famed Spartan army.[39] Even though they were not Christians, we share much in common with these ancient warriors. As we discussed in the last chapter, Ephesians 6 clearly explains that our enemy is not man, though he may be the source through which we encounter the enemy. Similarly, the Spartans believed their enemy not to be a flesh-and-blood opponent; instead, they believed it to be what they referred to as "the demons of the flesh." Particularly, the Spartans identified, above all else, that their primary enemy was fear.

Throughout a Spartan's lifetime, he might fight in hundreds of battles, but regardless of the opponent in battle, the enemy remained fear. They believed that to give in to fear and its effects is to give in to death; therefore, they did not train in preparation for the Persian army, or any other army for that matter. Instead, from the time they were born, they were trained to overcome fear.

This passage from *Gates of Fire* shows a dialogue between a Spartan boy and his mentor:

> "Answer this, Alexandros. When our countrymen triumph in battle, what is it that defeats the foe?"

> The boy responded in terse Spartan style, "Our steel and our skill."

> "These, yes," Dienekes corrected him gently, "but something more. It is that." His gesture led up the slope to the image of *Phobos* (god of fear).

> Fear.

> Their own fear defeats our enemies.

> "Now answer. What is the source of fear?"

> When Alexandros' reply faltered, Dienekes reached with his hand and touched his own chest and shoulder.

"Fear arises from this: the flesh. This," he declared, "is the factory of fear."[40]

We all experience fear on some level every day, whether consciously or subconsciously. We fear abandonment, not measuring up, rejection, punishment, pain, suffering, or loss. We fear being unloved, insignificant, or unnoticed. Many of us have felt fear while reading this book, as we wrestle with the idea that God might be calling us to radical levels of surrender—following Jesus down the narrow path that leads to life.

Fear is one of the fiercest enemies of faith, and while it is something Satan will most certainly seek to expose, fear finds its origins in the flesh. Fear (other than a reverent fear of God) is a byproduct of original sin.

After Adam and Eve ate the fruit from the Tree of the Knowledge of Good and Evil, their eyes were opened to their nakedness. Prior to this, God had been their covering, and in this they had found security. But in choosing sin, they chose to forgo this covering. It was lost, and along with it the comfort and security of God's love and protection.

For the first time they felt exposed, vulnerable, and afraid: "And they heard the sound of the LORD God walking in the garden in the cool of the day, and the man and his wife hid themselves from the presence of the LORD God among the trees of the garden. But the LORD God called to the man and said to him, 'Where are you?' And he said, 'I heard the sound of you in the garden, and I was afraid, because I was naked, and I hid myself'" (Genesis 3:8-10).

In the counseling world, studies have been conducted to categorize the psychological effects on children (starting in infancy) of parents that are present, loving, and affirming in contrast with those who are absent physically or emotionally, or perhaps are present, but abusive. Those who don't have the security of their parents' "covering" (love, care, protection, etc.) grow up with what is referred to as "insecure attachment." Essentially, this child grows up in a perpetual state of "unsafe."

As this child moves into adulthood, he (or she) often learns to manage this state of feeling "unsafe" by attempting to control his surroundings. He builds walls in the form of artificial comfort and security and conducts his life within the confines of his "control." As long as this control is maintained, he is able to function at a high capacity, but his innate fear is triggered whenever a variable is introduced that is outside his control and threatens to disrupt the safety he has constructed for himself. This often induces debilitating anxiety, volatile outbursts, and other irrational behaviors.

We have all been born into a sort of spiritual "insecure attachment." Innately we were created to be under a divine "covering," but sin divorced us from this creational intent. Subconsciously, we sense this absence. Like Adam and Eve, we know of our exposedness and our vulnerability; thus, fear has become deeply woven into the tapestry of who we are, causing us to exist in a perpetual state of "unsafe."

Intuitively, we know we are at odds with God. We understand that we are separated from his covering and his love, deserving of his wrath. As a result, we learn to hide. We attempt to construct an artificial semblance of safety, holding tightly to the reins of control. We believe if we could just navigate our lives in the right way, we could control our circumstances to avoid pain and suffering.

Through the cross, we have been restored once again under God's covering; he is our Provider and our Protector. But old habits die hard, and we often fail to live in light of this truth. Instead, we continue to let fear reign in our lives as we doubt the goodness and authenticity of God and his promises. Fear is the antitheses of faith; it is predicated on unbelief in the promises of God and in his goodness. It becomes a god we worship—*Phobos*.

"Not me," you say, "the only God I worship is Jesus." But anytime we make a decision or act out of fear instead of faith—anytime we cling to control of our circumstances—we are worshipping fear as our god. We are saying, "I love you God, but..." and then responding out of fear instead of the truth of his word and commandments.

The more we worship and serve this false god, the more we bar ourselves from experiencing the blessings of God's covering, and the harder our hearts become toward him because he threatens to impede upon the illusion of safety we have constructed by clinging to control when he asks us to surrender it. "No one can serve two masters, for either he will hate the one and love the other, or he will be devoted to the one and despise the other" (Matthew 6:24). You cannot serve both God and fear. Fear is one of the fiercest enemies of faith.

Often times our "faith" even plays into this desire for safety and control. Our Christianity becomes the means to the greater end of "feeling safe." It provides us a subculture that serves as a safety net to protect us from the "big scary world." We eat up the message that God loves us just the way we are, that he's pleased and proud of us, and that he wants to protect us from harm, danger, pain, and suffering. In this narrative we construct, God would never call us into something we would consider emotionally or physically dangerous, he would never ask us to suffer willfully, and it would never be part of his plan for us to experience pain. But despite the partial truths in these statements, this does not represent the God of the Bible. Perhaps it has become cliché, but it remains an important truth: "God is not safe, but he is good."

C.S Lewis illustrates this point quite clearly in *The Silver Chair* (a book in his series The Chronicles of Narnia):

"Are you not thirsty?" said the Lion.
"I am dying of thirst," said Jill.
"Then drink," said the Lion.

"May I — could I — would you mind going away while I do?" said Jill.

The Lion answered this only by a look and a very low growl. And as Jill gazed at its motionless bulk, she realized that she might as well have asked the whole mountain to move aside for her convenience. The delicious rippling noise of the stream was driving her nearly frantic.

"Will you promise not to — do anything to me, if I do come?" said Jill.

"I make no promise," said the Lion.

Jill was so thirsty now that, without noticing it, she had come a step nearer.

"Do you eat girls?" she said.

"I have swallowed up girls and boys, women and men, kings and emperors, cities and realms," said the Lion. It didn't say this as if it were boasting, nor as if it were sorry, nor as if it were angry. It just said it.

"I daren't come and drink," said Jill.

"Then you will die of thirst," said the Lion.

"Oh dear!" said Jill, coming another step nearer. "I suppose I must go and look for another stream then."

"There is no other stream," said the Lion."[41]

Jill wants the blessings of Aslan (the Christ-figure in the book), but without the risk, without disruption of her perceived safety, and without surrender of control; however, she cannot have it both ways. Aslan does not fit into what she wills for her life, the protections she has constructed, and the narrative she has created; he is outside of it, far too big to be contained by it. So the only way she gets to drink, the only way she doesn't die of thirst, is to draw near to the Lion in faith and trust.

The same is true of us. We desire to drink from God's streams of mercy and grace, but we want to hang on to control as we do. We want his benefits without having to trust him fully. We believe it's safer if we remain in control of our comfort and security, but there is no form of Christianity that does not require us to walk in faith and trust. Christianity requires that we surrender control. The only way we get to drink, the only way we don't die of thirst, is to draw near to God in faith and trust.

God is not "safe" in the same way we perceive safe to be. The truth is, that which we most need—which is ultimately best for us—might be quite painful in the moment. But there is no place that we are safer, in the truest sense of the word, than fully surrendered to his will, trusting our lives in the Father's hands. God has extended an invitation for us to come and freely drink from his streams, but we must do it on his terms, not our own.

This will require us to no longer serve the god of fear in our lives. Thankfully, fear has a kryptonite, and in this we have a Savior from fear's life-draining, faith-inhibiting grip.

This is where the Spartan story really gets good. As the warriors are sitting around a campfire while away at battle, one of the new members of the army asks one of the elders a very compelling question: if fear is the enemy, what is the opposite of fear? Not until the very end of the book is the answer revealed. Here is a portion of the explanation:

> "When a warrior fights not for himself, but for his brothers, when his most passionately sought goal is neither glory nor his own life's preservation, but to spend his substance for them, his comrades, not to abandon them, not to prove unworthy of them, then his heart truly has achieved contempt for death, and with that he transcends himself and his actions touch the sublime...."

> "Do you remember the night, Xeo, when we sat with Ariston and Alexandros and spoke of fear and it's opposite?"

> I said I did.

> "I have the answer to my question.... The opposite of fear," Dienekes said, "is love."[42]

Wow. I remember the first time I read that, being amazed how God could reveal such wisdom to me through a random piece of secular literature. Yet, this concept was in the Bible the whole time; I just hadn't recognized it—at least not in a way that transformed my heart.

1 John 4:18a reveals, "There is no fear in love, but perfect love casts out fear."

Love is the opposite of fear; it is its kryptonite. But while brotherly love, as Dienekes explained, is part of the equation, as Christians we have a far more powerful anecdote to drive out our fears: 1 John 4:8 explains that "God is love." God *is* love, and it is his love for us—his perfect love—that casts out all fears (4:18).

But how can we know this love is true? How can we trust that God loves us?

We can be confident of this love because of the cross, because God willfully chose to send Jesus to earth to die on a cross in our stead to demonstrate it. If we need proof of God's love for us, we needn't look further than Jesus' pierced and battered flesh hanging on an old splintery cross. 1 John 4:9-10 continues, "In this the love of God was made manifest among us, that God sent his only Son into the world, so that we might live through him. In this is love, not that we have loved God but that he loved us and sent his Son to be the propitiation for our sins."

God's love demonstrated on the cross is the key to eradicating our fear, and it does so in four primary ways. As we look closer at these concepts, I pray the Holy Spirit allows these truths to penetrate your heart in a transformative way.

1. <u>We Are Never Alone</u>

I was watching a television show awhile back about a comic book character named "The Flash." As his name implies, "The Flash" (Barry) has the incredible power to run really, really fast. Nonetheless, despite the acquisition of this incredible ability, Barry has a glaring weakness: fear.

As Barry is reflecting on his fear, he has a flashback to a memory of when he was a small child. As his mother (Nora) is tucking him into bed, young Barry tells her that he doesn't want her to turn off the lights because he is afraid of the dark. The following exchange proceeds:

> His mother asks, "If I turn this light off now, would you be scared?"
> "No," Barry softly responds.
> "That's because I'm here with you. See, you're not afraid of the dark, Barry; you're afraid of being alone in the dark and that goes away when you realize something. You're never really alone."[43]

Adam and Eve didn't experience fear until their sin spiritually disconnected them from their relationship with God. It was not their circumstances that scared them, it was being in their circumstances alone, without the covering of God's love.

The same is true of us. We aren't as afraid of the darkness, or of suffering, as we are of being alone in the dark—abandoned, left, forsaken. This is why God goes to such efforts to assure his people that he is with them. They are not alone, so they need not be afraid.

At the beginning of the book of Joshua, God's people are about to cross over the Jordan River and into the long-awaited Promised Land. Years earlier, spies had gone into the land and discovered "giants" heavily skilled in the proficiencies of war. The Israelites knew the obstacles they faced as they sought to inhabit the land. They knew the threat that awaited them on the other side of the Jordan—the odds that were stacked against them.

Undoubtedly, fear was a true and present reality in this moment. In fact, years prior, their ancestors allowed such fears to lead them into disobedience as they refused to follow God's command to enter this very land. Fear was perhaps the greatest danger to God's people in this moment, for it threatened their very faith in the promises of God.

Before the Israelites cross the river, God speaks these words of encouragement to Joshua: "Have I not commanded you? Be strong and courageous. Do not be frightened, and do not be dismayed, for the LORD your God is with you wherever you go" (Joshua 1:9).

God tells Joshua not to be afraid. Why? Because God will be with him wherever he goes, and this is his pledge to us as well.

In Hebrews 13:5, God promises, "I will never leave you nor forsake you," and, as Jesus commissions his disciples to take the Gospel to all nations, he assures them, "I am with you always, to the end of the age" (Matthew 28:20). Just as the commission to take the Gospel to all nations is for us, so is the promise that Jesus will be with us until the end of the age.

As Jesus prayed the night before his crucifixion in the Garden of Gethsemane, he was anxious to the point of sweating blood (Luke 22:39-44). Why was he anxious? Because on the cross, he would face the abandonment and forsakenness of God that we will never have to face precisely because he did so in our place. He feared what lay before him so that we might never have to fear what lies before us.

Jesus' death on the cross bridged the chasm created by our sin and restored us under the covering of God's love as his beloved children forevermore. Nothing can again separate us from the love of God.

We are afraid because we imagine a future without God in it. Because of Jesus and the cross, however, that future doesn't exist. When we realize we're never alone, we'll realize we never have to be afraid.

2. There is No Punishment in Love

Not only did Jesus take abandonment and forsakenness on our behalf, but he took the entirety of the punishment that the world's sins deserved. This means that no matter the number of times we fall short after becoming a Christian, God will never punish us for our sins. In this, we needn't fear the wrath of God; Jesus bore it on our behalf. 1 John 4:18b explains, "For fear has to do with punishment, and whoever fears has not been perfected in love."

Rather, God disciplines us in our sin, often by allowing us to experience the natural consequences of our behavior, *because* he loves us. Hebrews 12:3-11 explains:

> Consider him who endured from sinners such hostility against himself, so that you may not grow weary or fainthearted. In your struggle against sin you have not yet resisted to the point of shedding your blood. And have you forgotten the exhortation that addresses you as sons?
>
>> "My son, do not regard lightly the discipline of the Lord,
>>   nor be weary when reproved by him.
>> For the Lord disciplines the one he loves,
>>   and chastises every son whom he receives."
>
> It is for discipline that you have to endure. God is treating you as sons. For what son is there whom his father does not discipline? If you are left without discipline, in which all have participated, then you are illegitimate children and not sons. Besides this, we have had earthly fathers who disciplined us and we respected them. Shall we not much more be subject to the Father of spirits and live? For they disciplined us for a short time as it seemed best to them, but he disciplines us for our good, that we may share his holiness. For the moment all discipline seems painful rather than pleasant, but later it yields the peaceful fruit of righteousness to those who have been trained by it.

Nothing is more wounding than putting our faith and hope in anything other than Jesus—than treasuring lesser things and giving

THE IMPLICATIONS OF FAITH

way to sin. Conversely, nothing is more freeing and life-giving than learning to trust God entirely and completely in the midst of all circumstances, treasuring Jesus so mightily that even death is gain. This is the goal of the Lord's discipline. It is a sure testament of his unceasing love for us as his precious sons and daughters. It is always for our good, never to punish our sin.

We have a tendency to use discipline and punishment interchangeably, but we must learn the difference. Punishment is the debt to be paid following judgment—it is the sentencing for the offense. Discipline is a loving parent teaching a child to correct his or her behavior away from that which harms and toward what is for the child's ultimate good. There is no punishment in love.

3. <u>God Brings Beauty Out of Ashes</u>

Proverbs 3:14 says that wisdom is "more profitable than silver" and "yields a better return than gold." In fact, the entire summation of the first nine chapters of Proverbs is to explain the value and benefit of wisdom.

For the Christian, wisdom is a profound, heart-level understanding of the mysteries of the Gospel—God's deep love, grace, and mercy for us through Jesus' blood shed on Calvary—that leads to a transformed life. It is the key to peace and joy in the midst of even the most dire circumstances, predicated on the depth and breadth of truly knowing God in intimate relationship. Wisdom is unequivocal trust in his goodness, love, and sovereignty.

Psalm 46:1-3 (perhaps my favorite passage in all of Scripture) illustrates the fullness of this *Wisdom of God* in action:

> God is our refuge and strength,
>   a very present help in trouble.
> Therefore we will not fear though the earth gives way,
>   though the mountains be moved into the heart of the sea,

~ 198 ~

though its waters roar and foam,
  though the mountains tremble at its swelling.

Can you imagine this sort of apocalyptic scene? The earth is giving way and the mountains are falling into the sea; the waters are roaring and foaming and the mountains are trembling. I imagine the Psalmist on a small piece of land as everything around him literally falls apart, collapses, and crumbles. And yet, he does not fear. The Psalmist so deeply understands who God is and God's immense love for him that he is not afraid. Chaos surrounds him, but internally, he has peace.

This is the Wisdom of God in action. It is the essence of true freedom and joy as it transcends the need to control our circumstances in order to have peace. Rather, predicated on our deep knowledge and trust of God's love for us, it enables us to find peace regardless of the storms that rage around us.

As we talked about in chapter thirteen, God uses trials and tribulations to produce this type of deep-rooted trust in him. As I reflect on my own Christian journey, I am forced to admit that I have grown exponentially more in true wisdom during the "hard" times than during the "good" times. It is during these times that I am faced with the question, "Is God enough?" If everything else were stripped away, would knowing God intimately be enough to satisfy my deepest wanting? And each and every time (albeit often after much intense wrestling with God, this question, and many doubts), God has revealed himself to be abundantly sufficient. Consequently, the "worst" times of my life have also been the sweetest, and by far the most fruitful, seasons of my life, as I experienced intimacy with God in ways I had not previously known.

So if this type of knowing and trusting God is more valuable than silver and gold, and we grow in it exponentially more during the "bad" times than the "good," then we are forced to admit there is a strong sense in which the "bad" times are even better than the "good" because God uses them to give us the riches of himself. If the "bad" times yield such a profitable return, then what do we have to fear?

God promises he is working out everything "for the good of those who love him" (Romans 8:28 NIV). Thus, we needn't fear because whatever God brings into our lives, he will use for our ultimate good. If we are seeking a deeper intimacy with him in the midst of our trials, he will, without fail, use our suffering to accomplish that end.

In addition to God transforming us during the hard times so that we know and trust him more, there are times where he has plans to use our trials for a more tangible benefit. Consider the story of Joseph: he is sold into slavery by his brothers, who actually preferred him dead (Genesis 37:18-28). Then, he was wrongly accused by Potiphar's wife of making an advance at her and was thrown into prison for it (Genesis 39:1-20).

Nonetheless, he remained faithful, trusting in God's ability to use it for good—trusting that God's will was best; therefore, God allowed him to find favor with Pharaoh. Joseph was brought from prison to interpret a dream of Pharaoh's. From this, he was able to discern that Egypt would experience seven years of abundance followed by seven years of famine. In order to survive, they would need to store up grain for the next seven years (Genesis 41:1-36).

Joseph's ability to interpret the dream pleased Pharaoh, and he was appointed over all the kingdom so that only Pharaoh was greater (Genesis 41:39-45). Ultimately, Joseph was able to save the lives of many during the famine, including those of his own family. None of this would have been possible, however, if it weren't for the misfortunes he endured. In Genesis 50:20, Joseph tells his brothers, "As for you, you meant evil against me, but God meant it for good, to bring it about that many people should be kept alive, as they are today."

I heard a story on the radio several years ago that further demonstrates this sentiment: a disabled man in a wheelchair was seated in front of a store, with a bucket, trying to raise enough money to start a wheelchair basketball league. He had raised a few hundred dollars when some unruly teenagers robbed him, taking off with his bucket and all the money he had raised. He was heartbroken, and at first glance this seemed like a travesty, but God was at work in the storm.

A local news station caught wind of the incident and ran a story about it. This led to someone starting a GoFundMe page for him. By the time it was all said and done, more than $30,000 had been raised for this man and his basketball league.

God has the ability to bring beauty out of "ashes" every single time. This is most powerfully evidenced in the cross. God took the most horrible event in human history (the murder of the Son of God) and made it into the greatest event in human history (salvation for all those who would believe). There is not a circumstance we can encounter upon which God doesn't have the final word. Whether he uses it for our inner transformation as he brings us to a deeper knowledge and trust of him, a material purpose like in the case of Joseph (and the wheelchair story), or to "prepare for us an eternal weight of glory beyond all comparison" (2 Corinthians 4:17), we have God's promise that he loves us and is therefore working out all things for our good.

4. Our Love for Others Casts Out Fear

The Bible says we love because he first loved us. This has enabled us to love God, but also to love others in our lives with a Christ-like love. In fact, Jesus says this neighborly love is the second greatest commandment.

God has given us the ability and the command to love others, and like the Spartans, this love serves to overcome fear. When I was in the depths of my struggle with anxiety and depression, I had an opportunity through my personal training business to build deep relationships with clients. This would often lead to them sharing with me their struggles and sufferings, inviting me to speak into these things.

Even though I was not yet on the other side of my own struggles, I was able to share with my clients what God was teaching me and the work he was doing in me. I was able to use my pain to minister to them. Paul describes something similar in 2 Corinthians 1:3-4 (NIV): "Praise be to the God and Father of our Lord Jesus Christ, the Father of compassion and the God of all comfort, who comforts us in all our troubles, so that we can comfort those in any trouble with the comfort we ourselves receive from God."

I found that when I was helping other people with their pain, I got momentary reprieve from my own. I wasn't thinking about it or focusing on it; I was focused on my clients. As I loved and cared more about them than myself, I was able to momentarily escape the torments of my own mind.

I have heard it said that anxiety and depression are very narcissistic conditions. The self becomes so inwardly focused that it begins to collapse into a downward cycle of despair. This was true of myself. Yes, I had legitimate pains to grieve, but the anxiety and depression were primarily fear based and narcissistically fueled.

In John 15:12-13 Jesus tells his disciples, "This is my commandment, that you love one another as I have loved you. Greater love has no one than this, that someone lay down his life for his friends." As we learn to walk out our faith with this type of genuine love for others, we will be delivered from our fears and anxieties because it won't be about us anymore.

Perfect love casts out all fears.

Confronting Fear

For those who are in Christ, the chasm has been bridged, the debt has been paid, and the covering restored. We are benefactors of God's care, love, and protection. Yet, our propensity toward fear and our innate desire to control our circumstances persists. Thus, if we are going to allow the Gospel to overcome our fears, we must put our faith into action and confront them head-on.

Faith is an action based on a belief in what God says is true. We have explained in great detail the unbelievable truths of God's love for us and how they empower us to overcome fear, but we still have to put our faith in these truths. We still have to ask ourselves, "If I really believe in God's love, how then should I live?" We still have to jump.

Knowing these truths might not immediately deliver us from the *feeling* of fear, but it can deliver us from fear's control of our actions. It has been said, "Courage is not the absence of fear, but acting in spite of it."[44] The same can be said of faith. It is not the absence of fear, "but rather the assessment that something else is more important than fear."[45] It is the assessment that something is more true than the lies causing doubt. The feeling of fear will begin to dissipate the more we step out in faith and trust in God's love for us through Jesus Christ. Until then, faith calls us to act in spite of the presence of the feeling of fear by allowing his love to give us the courage and strength necessary to jump anyways.

Christian, are you on fire for God? Are you radically following in faith the leading of the Holy Spirit? Is the God of the Universe using you as a vessel to advance the kingdom and bring him glory? Most importantly, does your life evidence that which you claim to believe? If the answer is "no," I promise you, it is not God that is the problem; *Phobos* is the problem. Fear is the enemy. Love—God's love for us in Jesus Christ—is the answer.

CHAPTER 15 NOTES

[39] Steven Pressfield, *Gates of Fire*, (Bantam Dell, New York, 1998) 32. Excerpts used by permission.

[40] Pressfield. *Gates of Fire*, 32.

[41] THE SILVER CHAIR by C.S. LEWIS copyright © C.S. Lewis Pte. Ltd. 1953. Extracts reprinted by permission. (HarperCollins, New York, 1981), 557-558.

[42] Pressfield, *Gates of Fire*, 329, 331.

[43] *The Flash,* "The Man in the Yellow Suit," Directed by Ralph Hemecker. Written by Todd and Aaron Helbing. Warner Bros. December 9, 2014.

[44] Many attribute this quote to Mark Twain, but uncertainty about its origins remain.

[45] Franklin D. Roosevelt is credited with a similar quote regarding courage.

XVI.

SELF-PRESERVATION AND THE DEATH OF FAITH

S elf-preservation kills faith.

It seems logical to care for ourselves, doesn't it? We have an incredibly strong, natural inclination to survive, to care for ourselves, and to preserve our well-being. In fact, the Bible commands that we do so; self-care is not wrong. That's what makes the sin of self-preservation so hard to recognize, so subtle, and so deadly.

As Christians, we are called to lay down our lives—to follow in the footsteps of Christ, who took on suffering, even death, for the well-being of others. The one person who had the right to put his needs, his wants, and his well-being in front of others, laid down that right (Philippians 2:3-8).

As we tether ourselves to Christ in the sweet surrender of salvation, we are committing to following him wherever he leads. We have laid down the claim we have on our lives and entrusted them into the hands of our precious Savior. He leads; we follow.

As we set off on this journey with the Lord, there is often no conflict between the command to care for ourselves and the command to follow Jesus wherever he leads. The signs guiding and directing us on the path of life are often pointing in the same direction. Jesus: this way → Self-Care: this way →. But what about when we come to a fork in the trail? What happens when the sign reads, Jesus: this way ← Self-Care: that way →?

The sin of self-preservation occurs when we choose to prioritize our own well-being—our safety, our comfort, our provision, our plans, and even our very lives—over the leading of the Spirit and the commands of Jesus in Scripture. It seeks to predict the most favorable outcome—the one that keeps us the safest and most comfortable—and it seeks to put an asterisk by "doing right" if "doing right" has the potential to bring us hardship or pain. It justifies that Jesus would never ask us to lose our jobs, miss a meal, or risk our lives. It is perhaps the most basic instinct of our flesh and the most deadly to our faith and our witness to the rest of the world.

The Lord has called us to come and die, not just once, but daily in a series of small deaths over and over again (1 Corinthians 15:31). We no longer live for ourselves; we live for Christ (Romans 12:1). We no longer live for the kingdom of this world; we live for eternity. The Gospel flips the basic tenets of the world on their heads. In God's economy, down is up, last is first, suffering brings glory, and death is life.

In order for faith to be necessary, we must come to the proverbial fork in the road. It does not require faith to continue in the direction of what we evaluate to be in our own best interest. We do not need it to follow God when it benefits us in an overt way. Rather, the situations that require faith are when following Jesus asks us to forgo safety, security, comfort, and even our lives.

In the Bible, Esther comes to this fork in the road. A decree has been made to rid the land of Persia of all the Jews. Esther finds herself in a position where she could potentially influence the king and save her people. She has found favor in the eyes of King Xerxes and now resides inside the palace walls. The king is never to be disturbed, however; even Esther can only enter his presence if she is summoned. To approach him otherwise is punishable by death, unless he extends his scepter, pardoning her. So Esther has a decision to make. She can do what is right by the Lord and approach the king, risking her own life in an attempt to save her people, or she can choose the route of self-preservation.

In one of the finest examples of faith in all of Scripture, Esther responds, "If I perish, I perish" (Esther 4:16) and steps into the king's quarters. As many of us know, God uses Esther's act of faith to save the Israelite people. The king extends his scepter and grants her request that protection be decreed for her people.

I don't share this example to demonstrate that God will always come through and protect us from harm when we step out in faith. This isn't the case. What is best for us and the kingdom might be something very painful for us—even deadly (but because of Christ, death has taken on new meaning). No, I share this example because of Esther's heart posture: "If I perish, I perish." She was ready to die to do what was right. She stepped out in faith and left the consequences up to God. Do we possess the same heart posture?

Faith is like a muscle; it must be worked. If we want our faith to grow, we have to exercise it. We have to step out in faith. There is nothing scarier, and yet nothing will awaken a dormant or lukewarm faith more. As we step out in faith, the Spirit inside us is fanned into flame, and with it the cobwebs of complacency and apathy are shaken from our soul.

But what happens when we choose self-preservation instead of faith? The Israelites were faced with this question after being delivered out of slavery in Egypt. God leads them to the Promised Land—a beautiful land flowing with milk and honey. But as they approach, they send spies to scout out the land to see if it is really as God said. They determine that, while the land is extraordinary, the inhabitants of the land are too big and too powerful for them to take hold of it. Despite God promising the land to them and calling them to enter into it, they refuse because it is too dangerous, the risk too high. They choose self-preservation instead. As a result, the rest of their lives are spent wandering in the desert, never taking hold of what God had planned for them. What could have been an incredible opportunity to grow their faith as they tasted the goodness of the Lord ends up wasted (Numbers 13-14).

The same is true of us. Not only does faith fail to grow when we choose self-preservation, but it is actually smothered. The same Spirit who dwells inside us, who can be fanned into flame through faithful obedience, is also capable of being quenched. With every decision to act apart from the Spirit's leading—with every decision toward self-preservation—the Spirit inside us dims. Wherein passion and zeal once lived, complacency and apathy start to settle. We get stuck wandering in a spiritual desert, wondering what happened to the passion and zeal we once possessed. We wonder why God seems distant. Has he abandoned us?

No, dear Christian, if you are truly in Christ, God will never abandon you; however, your faith will flutter and flounder and the spirit of doubt will continue to grow as long as self-preservation is what governs your actions. Like the Israelites, you will find yourself stuck in a spiritual desert. And like the Israelites, you too will miss out on what God has planned for you—namely, knowing him with an intimacy foreign to most because you trusted him even in the face of certain hardship.

Unfortunately, self-preservation has other negative effects as well.

I was a lifeguard for several summers while I was in college. During training, our instructor taught us that a drowning person, in an effort to save himself, will push anyone in his vicinity under the water in order to stay afloat. In order to save his own life, he will drown whoever is closest by. Self-preservation is like that—if we treat it as our highest end, we will undoubtedly wound others in the process.

Recently, I witnessed a heartbreaking situation where self-preservation was the priority. False accusations were brought against a dear friend of mine. As the church leaders got involved, they chose to protect themselves above all else. To "rock the boat" would have put their jobs in jeopardy and threatened their well-being. Not wanting to "drown" themselves, they "drowned" a good man. As these Christian men—pastors and elders—chose self-preservation, my friend became the necessary sacrifice.

Self-preservation kills faith and often inflicts immeasurable wounds on the people for whom God has called us to die. But it's when we lay down this tendency to self-preserve and step out in faith that we find spiritual renewal and show the world the light and love of Jesus Christ.

We cannot follow after Jesus, and we *certainly* cannot reflect the type of radical, sacrificial love he demonstrated on the cross if we continue to place our own well-being above our commitment to Jesus. *Nothing* shows this world who Jesus is more than when Christians are willing to absorb pain so that those in their lives can avoid it, and *nothing* will grow our faith more than throwing off the sin of self-preservation and chasing after Jesus with reckless abandon.

This is faith: that in every decision we make, whether big or small, we hold tightly to nothing but Jesus, do right by him, and trust God with the consequences. Faithfully following after Jesus is our responsibility; the consequences belong to God. We can't anticipate the consequences and adjust our behavior based on what is most beneficial for us.

Instead, we simply do what's right and trust God with the rest: "If I perish, I perish."

XVII.

(FAUX) FREEDOM AND THE AMERICAN DREAM

Freedom—is there a word that stirs inside us more passion and pride than this? I know that, personally, something comes alive when I hear William Wallace's epic freedom speech in *Braveheart*[46]—or the one the President gives in the movie *Independence Day*[47]—and every Fourth of July, I seem to get goose-bumps (and even a little teary eyed) as the words from Lee Greenwood's classic "God Bless the USA" blast across the speakers in my car: "And I'm proud to be an American where at least I know I'm free..."[48] No, there's nothing quite like the idea of freedom—especially to those of us in the United States.

But freedom isn't just an American concept; it is a Christian one as well. The question, however, is whether the American concept of freedom and the Christian concept are the same, and, if they are not, what are the dangers of treating them as if they are?

John 8:34 tells us that everyone who sins is a slave to sin. Since we know that everyone has sinned and falls short of the glory of God (Romans 3:23), that means we were all once slaves to sin and spiritually dead. We were controlled by every desire in an effort to gratify our sinful nature, led by those desires into further destruction. We were "enslaved" in the truest sense of the word.

But God demonstrated his love for us in that while we were still sinners Christ died for us (Romans 5:8). Though we chose our enslavement by rejecting God, he deemed us worthy of rescuing; thus, he sent his Son to set us free. Galatians 5:1 (NIV) tells us, "It is for freedom that Christ has set us free." For those who have put their faith in Christ, the old, sinful nature is put to death and buried with Christ. We are born again, a new creation with a new nature, no longer a slave to sin. Jesus says, "So if the Son sets you free, you will be free indeed" (John 8:36). This is "freedom" in the truest sense of the word: forgiven and redeemed by the blood of Christ, risen a new creation in him.

But the Bible doesn't stop there. Romans 6:16-18 reads:

> Don't you know that when you offer yourselves to someone as obedient slaves, you are slaves of the one you obey—whether you are slaves to sin, which leads to death, or to obedience, which leads to righteousness? But thanks be to God that, though you used to be slaves to sin, you have come to obey from your heart the pattern of teaching that has now claimed your allegiance. You have been set free from sin and have become slaves to righteousness.

How does that make sense? How can we be both free and a slave at the same time? The answer is that Biblical freedom—true freedom bought for us on the cross by the blood of Jesus—looks a lot different from our "Americanized" version of it. Jesus tells us that true freedom comes from tethering ourselves to him and following after him. It results from surrendering our autonomy and self-will, not exercising it. He says true freedom comes when we surrender control of our lives, let him lead, and become slaves to Christ.

This, however, doesn't sound like the type of freedom we've come to celebrate in America.

According to the Declaration of Independence, we are born with certain inalienable rights afforded to us by our Creator: the right to life, liberty, and the pursuit of happiness. It is these rights, perhaps, that best embody what "freedom" means in the United States. We believe we have ownership over our lives, our actions, and our futures. We have a right to do and to pursue that which we think will make us happy. We have the right to total autonomy: to self-gain, self-promotion, self-provision, and self-preservation. It is from these ideals the "American Dream" was born.

The "American Dream" says that given the right political structure, freedoms, and opportunities, we can build for ourselves the lives we believe will make us happy, keep us safe, and bring us joy and contentment. With the right resources, if we work hard, we can meet all our perceived needs and desires.

It sounds great, doesn't it? But the problem is, this isn't what the Bible means when it speaks of "freedom."

Remember, we have an enemy in Satan, who wants nothing more than to destroy and devour us. He will use any means necessary to do so, even our culture, to alter our basic understanding of the word "freedom."

We are under attack, both personally and corporately, and we are in danger of allowing syncretism (creating a hybrid Christianity of what the Bible says and what the world says in a way that compromises Biblical truth) to drastically affect our spiritual health, our witness to the world, and threaten the very true freedom Christ died to secure. We have traded Biblical freedom for our Americanized version, and in doing so have re-enslaved ourselves all over again. We have bought the lie that the "American Dream" and our Christian faith can coexist, but in reality, we have divided our hearts as we seek to serve two masters.

This isn't a new problem; it's not unique to us. It is human nature to prioritize meeting our perceived needs over the mission of God, and it has been happening since the beginning of time.

We see this in the book of Haggai. The Israelites have returned from exile, and the temple has been destroyed. God tells the people to rebuild the temple, but they put it off for years, making excuses about why they need to take care of other things first. Haggai 1:2-6, 9 reads:

> "Thus says the Lord of hosts: These people say the time has not yet come to rebuild the house of the Lord." Then the word of the Lord came by the hand of Haggai the prophet, "Is it a time for you yourselves to dwell in your paneled houses, while this house lies in ruins? Now, therefore: Consider your ways. You have sown much, and harvested little. You eat, but you never have enough; you drink, but you never have your fill. You clothe yourselves, but no one is warm. And he who earns wages, does so to put them into a bag with holes. …You looked for much, and behold, it came to little. And when you brought it home, I blew it away. Why? Declares the Lord of hosts. Because of my house that lies in ruins, while each of you busies himself with his own house."

Do you see it?

"Because…my house…lies in ruins, while each of you busies himself with his own house" (Haggai 2:9).

That's the "American Dream" right there. That's what's happening now in the world, in our country, in our church, and in our own hearts. People's lives are falling apart; they are broken, hurting, hanging on by a thread, and desperately lonely. Some of them are sitting in our churches, and they're at our jobs, and they're in our neighborhoods. There are people taking their own lives because they're in so much pain. There are people dying out there, and they don't know Jesus. Yet, we're too busy with our own "house"—building the nice comfortable lives we want for ourselves—to even notice. We're too busy worrying about how we're going to entertain ourselves, which Netflix shows we're going to watch, or how we're going to renovate our homes. We don't have a temple anymore, but it's safe to say we're neglecting the mission of God for the same reason the people in Haggai were neglecting the temple.

Jesus says in Matthew 6:31-33 (NIV): "Do not worry, saying, 'What shall we eat?' or 'What shall we drink?' or 'What shall we wear?' For the pagans run after all these things, and your heavenly Father knows that you need them. But seek first his kingdom and his righteousness, and all these things will be given to you as well."

This is the exact opposite of the way the people behaved in the book of Haggai. The answer to what we actually need lies in dying to ourselves and surrendering to the mission of God, taking up our cross and following him.

What happens when we focus on our own "house" first? "You eat, but you never have enough; you drink, but you never have your fill. You clothe yourselves, but no one is warm. And he who earns wages, does so to put them into a bag with holes" (Haggai 1:6). We are never satisfied. Joy and contentment ever evade us, and we are emotionally and spiritually enslaved by our "freedom."

The issue isn't that the people in Haggai had paneled houses; it's that they prioritized their own houses, their own interests, and their own needs above the call and commands of God. It was a heart issue, and it still is for us. Freedom that is used to turn inward and focus on ourselves is no freedom at all; neither is freedom that is used to chase worldly comfort and security. Jesus tells us we cannot serve two masters—we will love one and hate the other (Matthew 6:24).

Freedom isn't doing whatever we want to or having personal autonomy. True freedom is when we surrender to Jesus and make him the Lord of our lives; it is when we repent of our self-obsession and start to live for Christ and for others. True freedom is found in Christ alone.

By all means, let us celebrate the freedoms we are so blessed to have in the United States—freedom from oppression, tyranny, and persecution. We should celebrate and be thankful. But as Christians, let us give further thought to the word "freedom." How are we stewarding it? Are we using it to serve the Lord or ourselves? Have we traded Biblical freedom for an Americanized version, re-enslaving ourselves all over again? Have we let autonomy and our "Christian freedoms" actually hinder us from following Jesus in faith?

If the Lord is leading you to repent of your self-serving ways, I pray you will make haste to heed this call and then celebrate all the more, for freedom is not just "stars and stripes" and "amber waves of grain." Freedom is a bruised and bloodied Savior and streams of his unceasing grace.

CHAPTER 17 NOTES

[46] *Braveheart,* directed by Mel Gibson, (1995; Icon Entertainment, (2004) dvd).

[47] *Independence Day,* directed by Roland Emmerich, (1996; Twentieth Century Fox, (2013) dvd).

[48] Lee Greenwood, *God Bless the USA,* You've Got a Good Love Coming (album), MCA, 1984.

XVIII.

DOCTRINAL PHARISEES

In many ways, I grieve the man I became while in seminary.

Allow me to explain. When I became a Christian at the age of seventeen, I experienced a wonderful reprieve from the depression, anxiety, loneliness, and restlessness I had experienced prior to salvation. I had a desire to get in the Word, go to church, participate in Bible studies, attend youth group meetings, etc. I was making new Christian friends. God was helping me battle sin in my life (i.e., lust, pornography, unwholesome talk, swearing, lying, cheating, and so forth).

But after a few years, the newness of it all wore off and my faith was relegated to a series of legalistic disciplines. For the most part, my faith was defined by what I didn't do, not by what I did. I didn't drink; I didn't cuss; I didn't have sex. I was a good guy—a good Christian who went to church and read his Bible. But for some reason, I was increasingly apathetic and lukewarm. The fire was fading, and many of my pre-salvation struggles were returning; specifically, the depression, the anxiety, and the pornography addiction.

Then one night it all changed. As I explained earlier, I was reading through my Bible (like a good Christian does) and I came to a passage in Acts that opened my eyes to the fact that I had been living a largely "Spirit-less" Christianity. The issue was not about healing people or speaking in tongues; rather, my eyes were opened by the fact that the Spirit was to be the presence of the living God, the Creator of the Universe, dwelling inside me, faithfully serving as a Teacher, a Counselor, and a Guide.

1 John 2:27 explains, "But the anointing that you received from him abides in you, and you have no need that anyone should teach you. But as his anointing teaches you about everything, and is true, and is no lie—just as it has taught you, abide in him." This coincides with the prophecy in Jeremiah 31:34, pointing to the New Covenant, which says, "And no longer shall each one teach his neighbor and each his brother, saying, 'Know the LORD,' for they shall all know me, from the least of them to the greatest, declares the LORD."

We won't need someone to teach us about the Lord because we will *know* the Lord!

Under the Old Covenant, the Israelites knew *about* the Lord; they had knowledge of him. They objectively knew information about him, as he had made it known to them. Subsequently, all this knowledge was formulated into a sort of "systematic theology." But the type of knowledge foretold in Jeremiah 31:34 was different: this knowledge would be intimate, like the knowledge between lovers. It would not be objective knowledge *about* God; it would be a personal knowledge *of* God (David and a few others in the Old Testament seemed to have this type of intimate knowledge, but it was not available to the people as a whole).

Following that night when I was reading Acts, I began to seek the Holy Spirit more intentionally. I wanted intimacy with God, and as I sought it, I found it. God began to bring the Scriptures to life. Instead of head knowledge, God began to write the Scriptures on my heart, and by doing so, began to transform me. Furthermore, there was a wonder and awe, the likes of which I had not known, as I walked out my daily life. I could sense the Lord's Presence with me wherever I went.

In many ways, the next several years were the hardest of my life. God was performing a sanctifying "surgery" in my life, removing idols, addictions, and attachments, while healing long-buried wounds. But at the same time, this was the sweetest season of my life because God was truly making himself known to me. I began to experience an intimacy with God I had never known before. Suddenly, I knew there was a distinct difference between knowing *about* God and *knowing* God, and I knew that no amount of intellectual ascent had the power to lead to intimacy. This does not mean that such intellectual pursuits are without benefit, but only that they are powerless in and of themselves.

We live in a strange time because of what technology has made possible; for example, I can tune into the daily life of nearly anyone on the planet through social media. I can look at pictures of a celebrity's life, family, leisure activities, workouts, food, and clothes. I can message this person directly, sometimes receiving a reply. I can tune in live as he or she shares a thought or performs a "Q-and-A session." All this can create the very powerful illusion that I know this famous person whom I have never actually met.

Technology has made it possible to know nearly as much objective information about a celebrity as you might know about your own family members and friends—maybe even more! I don't have the data to back this up, but I would be willing to bet that since the emergence of social media, cases of celebrity stalkers have drastically increased. The reason for this is that we can almost deceive ourselves into believing that these people are our friends—that we know them personally.

Conversely (and this might make me a bad husband), I just recently learned the color of my wife's eyes. Seriously, I actually had to double check what color they were before writing this (they're green, by the way). Come to think of it, I don't know her blood type either, nor could I tell you the make-up of her DNA. "But, Craig, don't you love your wife? How could you not know these facts?"

The answer is I desire to *know* my wife, not just to know about her. When I am looking into her eyes, I am not paying attention to the color. That's not my focus; I'm looking deeper. I want to connect with her in an intimate way—to see past the exterior and into the depths of her heart and soul because *objective knowledge does not equal intimacy*.

I may not know my wife's eye color or her blood type, but I do know her hopes and dreams, what she's afraid of, what she struggles with, what she's most ashamed of, and her biggest insecurities. I know where she is spiritually and what God is doing in her heart. I know how to comfort her after a hard day and how to make her smile when she's feeling down. I know her at her best and at her worst. I know my wife in deep and intimate relationship, and that will only continue to grow with each passing year.

So the question is, are you pursuing God like a social media stalker, reducing *knowing* him to a series of objective facts you've acquired about him? Or, instead, are you pursuing the type of intimate knowledge that occurs between two lovers? Are you drawing near to the *heart* of God through the Spirit by the blood of Jesus? Are you allowing yourself to be transformed by the truths you so eagerly pursue?

When I left for seminary, I *knew* God. I had deep relational intimacy with him on a daily basis. He was leading and guiding, teaching and instructing, convicting and comforting. He had brought such healing in my life and ignited a strong, persistent passion to share that with others. But then came the lectures and the assignments, the textbooks, and the Systematic Theology classes. Next, the foreign languages and the expensive words. After that came doctrine, confessions, creeds, eschatology, soteriology, ecclesiology, denominations, and tribal allegiances.

That was all well and good, but there was never any time to be transformed by this onslaught of "head knowledge." It was all I could do to keep up with the hundreds of pages of reading on a nearly daily basis and the constant essays and research papers. I accumulated knowledge upon knowledge; I kept learning more and more information, but there never seemed to be time to slow down and let a truth transform me. There was no time to be a "doer" of what I was hearing, putting into practice what I was learning.

I won't say that I didn't grow in certain ways during my time at seminary, or that I didn't learn a lot of very important information. I will say, however, that I did not grow in relational intimacy with God during that time. In fact, it was quite the opposite: when I graduated from seminary, I knew so much more about God, but I felt so much further from him. What once had been warm, familiar, and life-giving, was now cold and dry. Undoubtedly, I must shoulder some of the blame for this, as no one was stopping me from waking up before the sun came up to spend time in God's presence. My point is not to call for seminary reform (although I wouldn't be the first person to suggest substantial change is necessary), but rather to speak to a far more pervasive issue.

There exists in Christianity a new type of "Pharisee." This "Pharisee" is not legalistic in terms of adherence to outward works of the law, like the Pharisees in the New Testament were. Rather, this type of "Pharisee" is abrasively dogmatic in his doctrine and theology. This person has accumulated knowledge upon knowledge *about* God, but his life does not reflect the intimate *knowing* foretold in Jeremiah

31:34. His heart does not bear witness to being transformed by these truths.

Doctrinal "Pharisees" love to display their great learning and theological knowledge. They love to wave the banner of their tribe and to criticize other brothers and sisters in the faith. They are quarrelsome and divisive and love to argue and "talk down" to those who don't align with each of their theological convictions (even those that are secondary or tertiary issues). To them, each and every "doctrine" is a matter of life and death because they supposedly hold the authority of the Scriptures in such high regard. Doctrinal "Pharisees" must be right, prove they are right, and do so in view of many. But at what cost?

Love.

Love is often the casualty of the doctrinal "Pharisee's" affinity for truth and intellectual knowledge. 1 Corinthians 8:1-3 explains, "This 'knowledge' puffs up, but love builds up. If anyone imagines that he knows something, he does not yet know as he ought to know. But if anyone loves God, he is known by God." You see, divine knowledge apart from divine intimacy will always lead to divine misrepresentation. When our words are disconnected from the love of Christ, our words are "wrong" even when they're "right." We become a heretic of sorts. God is not glorified by our words or our extensive knowledge if that knowledge isn't saturated in love! The Bible is overwhelmingly clear on this.

1 John 3:16-18 explains: "By this we know love, that he laid down his life for us, and we ought to lay down our lives for the brothers. But if anyone has the world's goods and sees his brother in need, yet closes his heart against him, how does God's love abide in him? Little children, let us not love in word or talk but in deed and in truth."

Has God's love so saturated your being that this love flows out of you to the people around you?

In John 13:35 Jesus says, "By this all people will know that you are my disciples, if you have love for one another." And 1 Corinthians 13:1-3 reads: "If I speak in the tongues of men and of angels, but have not love, I am a noisy gong or a clanging cymbal. And if I have prophetic powers, and understand all mysteries and all knowledge, and if I have all faith, so as to remove mountains, but have not love, I am nothing. If I give away all I have, and if I deliver up my body to be burned, but have not love, I gain nothing."

We ought to seek to know the Bible thoroughly and to have good doctrine, *but* if it isn't producing in us the fruit of the Spirit ("love, joy, peace, patience, kindness, goodness, faithfulness, gentleness, self-control" (Galatians 5:22-23)) then we ought to keep our knowledge to ourselves until it does. For in this we are like the Pharisees who Jesus said "search the Scriptures because you think that in them you have eternal life; and it is they that bear witness about me [Jesus], yet you refuse to come to me that you may have life.... But I know that you do not have the love of God within you" (John 5:39-40, 42). In Matthew 23:15, Jesus further rebukes the Pharisees, who would disconnect the precepts of the law from its intended effects, promoting the letter of the law but missing the spirit of it entirely: "Woe to you, scribes and Pharisees, hypocrites! For you travel across sea and land to make a single proselyte, and when he becomes a proselyte, you make him twice as much a child of hell as yourselves."

C.S. Lewis has often been attributed as saying, "Education without values, as useful as it is, seems rather to make man a more clever devil."[49] I would add, "Theology without intimacy—without love—seems to make man the same." To the doctrinal Pharisee, knowledge is a loaded gun, or a double-edged sword, that is often wielded with little regard to who it is wounding.

Recently, a woman commented on a verse we posted on the social media site for an online ministry to which I contribute, but her comment revealed that she didn't understand the context of the verse. I won't tell you specifically what the verse was, but it was akin to taking Jeremiah 29:11 (NIV) out of context: "'For I know the plans I have for you,' declares the LORD, 'plans to prosper you and not to harm you, plans to give you hope and a future.'" Her understanding of it did not account for the context, nor was it heresy. It didn't say anything incorrect about God, but the particular verse at hand, taken in context, was not dealing with that truth. Within 30 minutes, a post by one of our followers showed up on our feed. This person had taken a screen shot of the woman's comments and posted it to their own feed with a condescending comment about the importance of context.

But imagine if she would have somehow come across this person's post? What if they had a mutual friend and word got back to her about it? How would that have made that woman feel? Was it necessary to belittle her and potentially make her feel small? Was the motivation of that action love? Could it not have instead been an opportunity to lovingly enter into a conversation with her and gently correct and teach, affirming her heart and intent, while instructing her to a better understanding? This is just a small sample of the plethora of examples I have witnessed by those puffed up on the knowledge of Christ, but lacking the love of Christ, as evidenced by the gifts of the Spirit.

Sadly, I too have been guilty of this. Nearing the end of my time in seminary, my wife and I along with a few friends took a "vision" trip to Huntington Beach, California, to discern the Lord's calling regarding church planting in that location. My friend and I scheduled several meetings with local pastors to gauge the culture and spiritual climate of the area. As we went into these meetings, shamefully, my posture was one of pride. I was puffed up on my intellectual knowledge, and as a result, I entered the meetings with a cynical, critical, judgmental, and ultimately, pharisaical attitude. I was looking for what these pastors/churches were doing wrong, and congratulating myself on how much better we would do it. In my mind, these men just didn't understand the Bible, theology, ministry, and specifically ecclesiology quite like we did. In three short years I had become the very thing I hated: prideful and self-righteous in the name of Christ.

Christian, do you spend more time accumulating knowledge than you do being transformed by it? Do you come to God's word to learn more than you do to meet with God and be changed? Do you spend more time studying theology than you do broken by your failure to love those in your path with the love of Jesus?

Does truth matter? Without a doubt. We must be unwavering in our claim that "there is salvation in no one else, for there is no other name under heaven given among men by which we must be saved" (Acts 4:12). We must be steadfast in the truth that we are saved by grace through faith alone, not by works, but by the free gift through Jesus Christ (Ephesians 2:8-9). By all means, we should continue to learn; however, we ought to seek to be transformed by what we are learning before we continue to pile knowledge upon knowledge. By all means, let us hold to right doctrine, but not at the expense of what right doctrine ought to produce: Christ-like love.

In Galatians 5, Paul is making the argument for why Christians needn't become circumcised before becoming a Christian as the religious leaders were advocating. His reasoning is this: "For in Christ Jesus neither circumcision nor uncircumcision has any value. The only thing that counts is faith expressing itself through love" (Galatians 5:6, NIV). You see, the precepts of the faith never trump the onus to love; what counts is faith expressing itself through love. Just a few verses later Paul adds, "For the whole law is fulfilled in one word: 'You shall love your neighbor as yourself.' But if you bite and devour one another, watch out that you are not consumed by one another" (Galatians 5:14-15). We are never exempt from prioritizing love above all else. Remember, it was the "good" Samaritan that Jesus exalted because he exemplified the love of God, not the Pharisee with the "right" theology (Luke 10:37).

A harsh or unloving Christian is not only a contradiction, but an abomination. Will we fall short of a Christ-like love in our daily lives? Without a doubt we will, and there is grace for those like us, but let that not be the way we are known. Instead, let it be true of us that they will know that we are Christians, not by our great learning, but by our great love (John 13:35).

And that brings me to my final point. Often times a doctrinal "Pharisee" will claim the most loving thing he can do is be truthful with someone, and this is quite true. Proverbs 27:6 says, "Faithful are the wounds of a friend; profuse are the kisses of an enemy." But is the truth we are speaking occurring in the context of a loving friendship? Furthermore, God's word commands us to speak the truth in love (Ephesians 4:15), and as Colossians 4:6 says, "Let your speech always be gracious, seasoned with salt, so that you may know how you ought to answer each person." How we say what we say is as important as the words we speak; love and tact matter.

As we seek to grow in the Lord while following him on this pilgrimage, let us be wary of this enemy of faith: a puffed-up knowledge that masquerades as spiritual maturity. May we be repentant of having knowledge of God's word but not putting it into action or allowing it to transform us.

CHAPTER 18 NOTES

[49] It remains unclear if Lewis actually said this. While it does not come from *The Abolition of Man* as is often attributed, it does embody several sentiments put forth by Lewis in this and other works.

PART V:
FAITH MADE COMPLETE

The Bible tells us that Abraham's faith was made complete by his obedience, as he implemented his belief in a tangible way (James 2:22). And yet, Hebrews 12:2 tells us that Jesus is the Author and Perfecter of our faith. Which is true?

The answer is both, existing in a perfect, inseparable, God-ordained tension.

As we move into the last section of the book, it is paramount that we grasp fully both of these essential elements of the Christian faith. We are called to make our faith complete by responding by faith in everything we do—by living out the implications of what we claim to believe. Nonetheless, we will stumble and fall as we make these efforts; thankfully, we have an Advocate in Jesus, who, as the Perfecter of our faith, fills in what is lacking.

XIX.

THE NATURE OF THE RACE

The Leadville Trail 100 is one of the most grueling foot races in the world. This one-hundred-mile ultra-marathon takes place in Leadville, Colorado—the highest elevated town in all of North America. At two miles above sea level, Leadville is nearly inhospitable. In the winter months, it gets so cold that the fire department won't ring the bell for fear it will shatter, and the depleted oxygen from the high altitude makes simply being alive an intense cardiovascular exercise. Only the most elite in endurance performance are able to finish the race. It's not enough just to be conditioned; you have to be tough, really tough. [50]

Author Christopher McDougall says of the race:

To get a sense of [how challenging it is], try running the Boston Marathon two times in a row with a sock stuffed in your mouth and then hike to the top of Pikes Peak.

Done?

Great. Now do it all again, this time with your eyes closed. That's pretty much what the Leadville Trail 100 boils down to: nearly four full marathons, half of them in the dark, with twin twenty-six-hundred-foot climbs smack in the middle. Leadville's starting line is twice as high as the altitude where planes pressurize their cabins, and from there you only go up.

....

Leadville racers routinely fall off bluffs, break ankles, suffer overexposure, get weird heart arrhythmias and altitude sickness.... Less than half the field makes it to the finish every year.[51]

In his bestselling book *Born to Run*, McDougall chronicles the race over a few-year span in the early 1990s. His interest over this particular period centers around the participation of a mystery tribe of "running people" discovered deep in Mexico's deadly Copper Canyons: the Tarahumara Indians. Legend is told of the Tarahumaras' ability to run hundreds of miles at a time without rest or injury. At the Leadville Trail 100, the developed world would get an opportunity to see if the legend was true.

Despite the nearly god-like hype surrounding the Tarahumaras, there was one challenger determined to give them a run for their money.

Ann Trason was little, but she was full of spunk, fight, and determination. Oh, and she was a heck of an ultra-marathon runner, having dominated nearly every race in which she had taken part. Many (Ann included) believed the Tarahumaras had met their match.

As the starting gun fired, the top Tarahumaras (Martimano and Juan) immediately shot to the front of the pack. Far from pacing themselves for a twenty-hour race, they began at a near impossible speed. Ann would *not* be outdone, however, so she steadied in at a pace just behind them, waiting for just the right time to push past them.

By mile forty, Ann had done just that. By mile sixty, she had built a twelve-minute lead, and by mile seventy-two, it was stretched to twenty-two minutes. But then it happened: at mile ninety, with just ten miles remaining, the younger Tarahumara runner, Juan, made his move. McDougall tells the story:

> It was just past eight in the evening and the woods around her were sinking into darkness—and that's when something burst out of the trees behind her. It came on her so fast, Ann couldn't even react; she froze in place in the middle of the trail, too startled to move, as Juan darted to her left with one stride and back onto the trail with the next, his white cape swirling around him as he whisked past Ann and disappeared down the trail.
>
> *He didn't even look tired! It's like he was just...having fun!* Ann was so crushed, she decided to quit. She was less than an hour from the finish line, but the Tarahumara joyfulness...had totally disheartened her. Here she was, absolutely killing herself to hold the lead, and this guy looked like he could have snatched it any time he pleased.[52]

You see, there are two different ways to run a race.

Ann ran from a deficit. She felt as if she had to prove something. Did she love running? Sure, but she also loved proving people wrong. When her husband called her a wimp during a training run up a big hill, she became determined to become a better hill runner than he was.[53]

She also *hated* losing; you could even say she feared it. Part of her strategy in running the Leadville Trail 100 was to get out in front early and let the fear of being passed by another competitor give her the extra drive she needed.[54] It would not be a stretch to ascertain that Ann tied her self-worth to her performance. Winning affirmed her; losing...well, losing did the opposite.

THE IMPLICATIONS OF FAITH

But the Tarahumara were different: they didn't run from a deficit. They didn't feel as if they had anything to prove or anything to earn. They weren't worried about winning or losing; they just loved running; it's who they were: *the running people.* They ran out of their identity, and because of this, they ran with joy. They ran with contentedness:

> 'Such a sense of joy!' marveled Coach Vigil, who'd never seen anything like it. 'It was quite remarkable.' Glee and determination are usually antagonistic emotions, yet the Tarahumara were brimming with both at once, as if running to the death made them feel more alive.[55]

Christian, you also have a race to run. From the moment you repented and believed, your life on this earth became a race, and Jesus became the prize. Hebrews 12:1 explains, "Therefore, since we are surrounded by so great a cloud of witnesses, let us also lay aside every weight, and sin which clings so closely, and let us run with endurance the race that is set before us." And in 1 Corinthians 9:24-27, Paul states:

> Do you not know that in a race all the runners run, but only one receives the prize? So run that you may obtain it. Every athlete exercises self-control in all things. They do it to receive a perishable wreath, but we an imperishable. So I do not run aimlessly; I do not box as one beating the air. But I discipline my body and keep it under control, lest after preaching to others I myself should be disqualified.

We have a race to run, but understanding the nature of this race is of the utmost importance.

Paul explains this nature in Philippians 3:7-14 (emphasis added):

> But whatever gain I had, I counted as loss for the sake of Christ. Indeed, I count everything as loss because of the surpassing worth of knowing Christ Jesus my Lord. For his sake I have suffered the loss of all things and count them as rubbish, in order that I may gain

Christ and be found in him, not having a righteousness of my own that comes from the law, but that which comes through faith in Christ, the righteousness from God that depends on faith—that I may know him and the power of his resurrection, and may share his sufferings, becoming like him in his death, that by any means possible I may attain the resurrection from the dead.

Not that I have already obtained this or am already perfect, but I press on to make it my own, because Christ Jesus has made me his own. Brothers, I do not consider that I have made it my own. But one thing I do: forgetting what lies behind and straining forward to what lies ahead, I press on toward the goal for the prize of the upward call of God in Christ Jesus.

So Paul essentially says, "Because Jesus has made me his own, I run this race in pursuit of holiness (righteousness and obedience)—in pursuit of Jesus himself. Running the race—forsaking all things to follow Jesus—is what it means to have faith in Christ." But then he follows it up with one of the most encouraging verses in all of Scripture. Paul concedes, "Not that I have already obtained this or am already perfect..." (Philippians 3:12).

You see, Paul is a new creation in Christ. He has a new nature. He is a child of God—filled with the Holy Spirit. He has forsaken all, not just to follow Jesus, but to *run* after him. He has sacrificed, suffered, toiled, and strained, but even in all of that, he is not able to live perfectly. As he runs this race of Christian discipleship, chasing after Jesus with everything he has, he never graduates beyond a need for grace; he still stumbles and falls down. He still sins—yet to attain that for which he toils (the full realization of his justification and sanctification).

Grace empowers his efforts toward being Christ-like, and it is grace when those efforts are successful. But, most importantly, Paul is free to run without fear because if he falls down, grace is right there to pick him back up again. When he does fall, he doesn't beat himself up, he doesn't quit, and he certainly doesn't use a theology of cheap grace to reason that since Jesus already "ran" for him, he needn't run in the first place. No, Paul simply gets back up and "forgetting what lies behind (he forgets about the failures) and straining forward to what lies ahead, [he] presses on toward the goal for the prize of the upward call of God in Christ Jesus" (Philippians 3:13-14).

Radical Grace

It was late evening several years ago. I was living alone for the first time in my life, so the temptation to look at pornography had been heightened. I was going through a difficult season. I was experiencing very real spiritual warfare, having constant battles with depression and anxiety, and struggling with restlessness and discontentment. But even in the midst of all this, I felt as if I was growing in my faith. After a few months of really struggling with pornography, I had finally put together a stretch of time where I didn't mess up. One particular night, however, I was especially depressed. I was heartbroken over a friendship with a girl, which had ended, along with my hopes of it becoming something more. As I had countless times before, I turned to pornography to try to medicate the pain.

There was a very strong part of me that didn't want to do it. I knew I shouldn't. I even knew the falsehood of the lies the addiction was promising to satisfy, but I began down that path of destruction anyway, fully aware of what I was doing, yet unable to stop myself.

I messed up, and I gave into the temptation. I looked at pornography, and I did what one generally does while looking at it. Then I began experiencing the consequences. The pain I was feeling before I messed up didn't come close to how I felt afterward. All that pain and hurt was still there but with an added level of guilt, shame, and brokenness that was almost more than I could bear. Satan, also known as the Accuser of the Brethren, began a full-fledged assault and the voices started in: "You're such a failure. You're pathetic. You're a terrible person. You call yourself a Christian?"

That night after I messed up, I already knew I was going to do it again the next day. This was fairly common for me; rarely would I mess up as an isolated event. Instead, once I headed down that path and gave into temptation that one time, I would usually end up binging with pornography four or five times over the next few days. The cycle looked like this: I would mess up, then experience an incredible amount of guilt and shame. As a result of the shame, I would draw into isolation, where I would be a sitting duck for Satan's lies. It would be very easy for him to convince me to fall again, and I would, usually several more times before the self-loathing reached such a pinnacle that I would be driven to my knees, repenting of my sin, and promising God I would try harder.

I did look at pornography again the next day, but what happened next changed my life and my understanding of the Gospel forever. I sat there after I finished, waiting for the brief moment of ecstasy to subside and the shame and the guilt to come in full force. Only this time, it didn't come; instead, a peace came over me that I can't fully describe. In that moment, God whispered to me, "You are forgiven. It is finished. I love you." As I began to cry, I fell to my knees and worshipped the Lord. Even as I retell this story now, I am moved to tears. I am moved to worship.

Now this in no way undermines what we talked about in chapter eight. Our sin *should* deeply grieve us. God wasn't teaching me that I shouldn't be broken by my sin, or that I shouldn't feel pain when I fall short of living my life fully surrendered to him. Remember, this is evidence of a heart set on pleasing him, and God has sanctifying purposes for such pain. Rather, that night, God was revealing to me through the Holy Spirit a deeper understanding of just how radical the Gospel is. I am forgiven—not just a little bit, not just partially, not just if I don't ever look at pornography again. No, I am completely and totally forgiven and justified before God in Christ Jesus. Every sin—past, present, and future—has been paid for in full. It is finished. As Romans 8:1 so joyously proclaims, "There is therefore now no condemnation for those who are in Christ Jesus."

Jesus died so I could look at porn. That's a pretty raw statement. That's a pretty difficult statement to understand—one that would sound really bad if taken out of context—but it is a true statement. Jesus died so I could look at porn. That doesn't mean I *should* look at porn; we've already discussed all the negative consequences of sin. But it does mean that—*as I am genuinely seeking to fight sin and live for Jesus*—if I do look at porn or sin in some other way, I am still saved. I am still forgiven. I am still loved. As Romans 8:38-39 states, "I am sure that neither death nor life, nor angels nor rulers, nor things present nor things to come, nor powers, nor height nor depth, nor anything else in all creation, will be able to separate us from the love of God in Christ Jesus our Lord."

I am eternally forgiven and eternally secure in Jesus. From here on out, my sin will never separate me from the love of God because all of my filthy sin was put on Jesus, nailed to a cross, and stricken by the wrath of God; and all of Jesus' perfect fulfillment of the law has been credited to me.

That's the message of the Gospel. Isn't it radical?

In seminary, I had a professor who would always say, "The indicatives empower the imperatives." What this means is that the truth of the Gospel, the truth that we have been united with Christ by his blood, empowers us to obey that which God has commanded us to do. The commandments are still imperatives, and we are still called to obedience and holiness, but we can't put the cart before the horse. The imperatives never serve to earn the indicatives. We only put forth effort in *response* to grace, not to earn it. We have a race we *must* run (the very definition of faith implies it), but if we try to run this race apart from being saturated in Gospel understanding, we run it in vain.

For the Tarahumara, not to run would be contrary to their nature—an offense to it even. To those of us who claim to be followers of Christ but fail to make every effort to walk in his ways, the same is true: it is an offense to our nature.

"Running people" run. Christians follow Jesus in faithful obedience. But as we "run this race," we do so out of our identity as children of God, saved and sustained by the grace of Jesus. We never do it to earn approval, affirmation, love, or forgiveness. Out of this grace, the child of God learns to run like the Tarahumara—with the perfect blend of two seemingly antagonistic emotions, glee and determination.

Paul was able to strive, strain, and press on toward the goal, all the while knowing that whatever it cost him to run the race paled in comparison to the glory and joy of knowing Jesus as he ran.

This is the "nature of the race" of the Christian faith: we strive, strain, and press on toward Jesus as the prize, running with Jesus by our side, empowered and sustained by the good news of God's grace through Jesus Christ crucified for the forgiveness of our sins. We must never lose sight of this.

The writer of Hebrews, right after imploring us to run with endurance the race marked before us, instructs us to do so by "looking to Jesus, the founder and perfecter of our faith, who for the joy that was set before him endured the cross, despising the shame, and is seated at the right hand of the throne of God" (Hebrews 12:2).

Christian, your faith will be imperfect. But take heart, for Jesus is both the Founder and Perfecter of our faith; therefore, let us set our eyes upon Jesus, and let us set our feet to running after him with all of our hearts, all of our souls, and all of our minds.

CHAPTER 19 NOTES

50 Excerpt(s) from BORN TO RUN: A HIDDEN TRIBE, SUPERATHLETES, AND THE GREATEST RACE THE WORLD HAS NEVER SEEN by Christopher McDougall, copyright © 2009 by Christopher McDougall. Used by permission of Alfred A. Knopf, an imprint of the Knopf Doubleday Publishing Group, a division of Penguin Random House LLC. All rights reserved. (Vintage Books, New York, 2011), 57-61.

51 McDougall, *Born to Run*, 60.

52 Ibid., 103.

53Ibid., 86.

54 Ibid., 84.

55 Ibid., 91.

XX.

LIVING MARTYRS

"**Y**eah, but did you die?"

These words hang on the wall of the gym where I work as a personal trainer. They are meant to incite humor—making light of our sometimes dramatic overreactions to a really challenging workout. And yet, this seemingly innocuous phrase ought to be one that every professing Christian reckons with, for that is exactly what we are called to do as Christians: we are called to die.

On February 15, 2015, the radical Islamist group ISIS released a video to the worldwide media showing the gruesome beheading of twenty-one Egyptian Christians. The video was titled "A Message Signed With Blood to the Nation of the Cross." It was meant to drive fear into the hearts of billions of Christians worldwide, intimidating them into abandoning their faith in the One called Jesus. It was meant as a threat and a warning and to make the Christians look weak and pathetic.

In the weeks following the brutal attack, reporters were able to learn more about these twenty-one men. They were young (in their twenties), and most had families. Living under the poverty line in Egypt, they had traveled to Libya in search of work to help feed their families. While in Libya, the men were captured when their bus was stopped by the terrorist group. Over the next several weeks, it is reported that several of the men were tortured as ISIS attempted to get them to deny Christ as their Savior in exchange for their lives. Not one of the men caved; none were willing to deny Jesus.

As it became clear to ISIS that these men would not be converted, it was decided they would die. The twenty-one men were led in a single file line onto a beach by their captors, who were dressed in black, wearing masks, and wielding knives. Kneeling down, with knives to their throats, their death a foregone conclusion, the men can be heard in the video singing praises to Jesus and proclaiming his precious name as their lives are taken. These men died as martyrs, killed because they followed Jesus.[56]

Given where we live, there is a good chance that none of us will be faced with a situation like the twenty-one Egyptian martyrs, but this hasn't always been true (nor is it currently true in many parts of the world today).

For the first- and second-century Christian, the prospect of martyrdom was ever present. The killing of Christians for their faith began almost immediately following Jesus' crucifixion and the dispensing of the Holy Spirit at Pentecost. Acts 7:54-60 tells of the stoning of Stephen, the first Christian martyr, as he is testifying that Jesus is the Christ:

> Now when they heard these things they were enraged, and they ground their teeth at him. But he, full of the Holy Spirit, gazed into heaven and saw the glory of God, and Jesus standing at the right hand of God. And he said, "Behold, I see the heavens opened, and the Son of Man standing at the right hand of God." But they cried out with a loud voice and stopped their ears and rushed to-

gether at him. Then they cast him out of the city and stoned him. And the witnesses laid down their garments at the feet of a young man named Saul. And as they were stoning Stephen, he called out, "Lord Jesus, receive my spirit." And falling to his knees he cried out with a loud voice, "Lord, do not hold this sin against them." And when he had said this, he fell asleep.

Acts 8 tells us that Saul (the Apostle Paul prior to his conversion) approved of the execution (vs. 1), and continued to go door to door to round up as many Christians as he could to throw them into prison (vs. 3). It is likely that many of these Christians experienced the same fate as Stephen.

Acts 12:1-3 reads, "About that time Herod the king laid violent hands on some who belonged to the church. He killed James the brother of John with the sword, and when he saw that it pleased the Jews, he proceeded to arrest Peter also."

While Peter would escape death for the time being, Jesus had promised him long before that being a disciple would cost him his life (John 21:18). Peter would eventually be crucified in Rome under the reign of Nero (A.D. 54-68) for his faith (it is alleged that he asked to be crucified upside down because he believed himself to be unworthy to be crucified in the same manner as the Lord Jesus).

But Nero didn't stop there—he had made it his personal plight to rid society of as many Christians as he could and to do so in the most horrific manner imaginable. The Roman historian Tacitus, in his book *Annals*, wrote:

> Therefore, to stop the rumor [that he had set Rome on fire], he [Emperor Nero] falsely charged with guilt, and punished with the most fearful tortures, the persons commonly called Christians, who were [generally] hated for their enormities.... Accordingly first those were arrested who confessed they were Christians; next on their information, a vast multitude were convicted, not so much on the charge of burning the city, as of "hating the human race."

In their very deaths they were made the subjects of sport: for they were covered with the hides of wild beasts, and worried to death by dogs, or nailed to crosses, or set fire to, and when the day waned, burned to serve for the evening lights. Nero offered his own garden players for the spectacle....[57]

With the exception of Judas (who hanged himself after betraying Jesus) and John (who was reportedly boiled alive by his persecutors but was exiled to the island of Patmos when he didn't die), the rest of the twelve disciples were martyred for their faith, along with a great multitude of other early Christians. It wasn't until Constantine converted to Christianity in A.D. 312 and subsequently decriminalized Christian worship that Christians experienced a reprieve from the persecution that had defined so much of their history up until that point.[58]

Nevertheless, Christian martyrdom has never fully ceased. In various parts of the world throughout history, there have always been Christians for whom simply claiming the name of Jesus is a death warrant. It is with *this* understanding that we must read Jesus' insistence that we count the cost of following him. It is with *this* understanding that we must read Jesus' invitation to deny ourselves, take up our cross, and follow him, saving our lives by willfully losing it.

Dietrich Bonhoeffer famously contends, "When Christ calls a man, he bids him come and die."[59] Christian, it is this message I wish to leave you with as this journey through *The Implications of Faith* comes to a close: the call to follow Jesus is a call to die.

Biblically, there is no such thing as half-hearted discipleship or being moderately surrendered to Christ. As Charles Spurgeon explains, "If Christ is not all to you he is nothing to you. He will never go into partnership as a part savior of men. If he be something, he must be everything, and if he be not everything, he is nothing to you."[60] David Platt adds, "We are settling for a Christianity that revolves around catering to ourselves when the central message of Christianity is actually about abandoning ourselves."[61]

In the first-century, Christians had to willfully resolve that they were willing to die to follow Jesus. It was not hyperbole for them to talk about "taking up their cross." In a very real way, they were forced with confronting the reality of death, to stare it in the face, and decide "Jesus is worth it; he is better," knowing full well at any moment they might be captured, imprisoned, tortured, or killed; that beheading, crucifixion, being burned at the stake, or any number of other torturous deaths could be just around the corner.

By being confronted with this reality, having to truly consider such ultimate costs, these early Christians "died" long before they became martyrs. At the moment of decision to follow Jesus, these men, women, and children were willfully surrendering every claim they had on their lives into the Father's hands.

We may never have to physically die because of our faith in Jesus. While this is cause for rejoicing, we do ourselves a disservice to consider the cost of following Jesus any less severe for us than it was for the early Christians. We have accepted the lie that we can be "Christians" without having to count the cost, without having to forsake *everything* to follow after him, and without having to die. As A.W. Tozer puts it, "A whole new generation of Christians has come up believing that it is possible to 'accept' Christ without forsaking the world."[62]

Close your eyes with me and imagine it is the first century. Nero is the leader of Rome, Christianity is despised by the Romans and the Jews (it is blasphemy to the Jews and a threat to the Romans), and it is illegal to gather in Christian worship. Persecution is widespread; martyrdom is common. You have just heard the Gospel message for the first time and are cut to the core. Your eyes are open to see that Jesus is Lord, and your conscience is ablaze. You are fully aware that you are a sinner deserving of hell—that to repent and believe in Jesus is the only way to be saved—yet, fully aware that to do so might cost you your life. What would you do? Would you still profess Christ? Would you forsake all to follow Christ?

We might claim to be Christians. We might have prayed a prayer asking Jesus into our hearts. Perhaps we regularly go to church, hang out with Christian friends, read our Bibles, and pray; we might even know all the doctrines of the Bible. If we have not "died" with Christ by taking up our cross, however, we cannot live with him, now or eternally.

There is a scene in the television series *Band of Brothers* where one of the brave and heroic soldiers (Capt. Ronald Speirs) is addressing a more cowardly one (Blithe). Speirs explains, "Blithe, the only hope you have is to accept the fact that you're already dead, and the sooner you accept that, the sooner you'll be able to function as a soldier's supposed to function."[63]

The same is true for us: we cannot live for Jesus until we have died to the world, died to our wills, died to our comfort and security, and died to living to preserve our lives. Only then will we be truly free and able to walk in faithful and joyful obedience to Christ. Until then, we will be double-minded in everything we do, claiming to believe in Jesus and yet living in a way that suggests otherwise.

We might never have to physically die for our faith, but we must wrestle with the prospect of doing so. We must get to that point where we are ready and willing, for every one of us is called to be a living martyr, resolved to follow Jesus wherever he may lead and whatever it may cost. This is what it means to truly take up your cross and follow Jesus.

We are in desperate need of revival, both personally and corporately, but that doesn't happen until we wrestle with this one question: "Yeah, but did you die?" We cannot live for Jesus in faith until we can answer "yes" to this question.

In John 14:6, Jesus says, "I am the way, and the truth, and the life. No one comes to the Father except through me." He is saying, "Life is found in me and nothing else." We are right to value life, but here Jesus redefines it for us. Life is not the breath in our lungs, the blood in our veins, or the beat of our hearts; life is being reunited with God, through Jesus, as we were created to be. Jesus is life, and as we step out in faith, believing this is true, we will ignite a fire in our own hearts by which we will set the world ablaze with the light and love of Jesus Christ.

Of those men from Egypt (from the story at the beginning of the chapter), twenty of the twenty-one were Christians when they walked onto the beach; the twenty-first guy was not. He had simply been traveling with them, looking for work. On the beach, after the first twenty men had been beheaded because they would not deny Christ, this man was given the opportunity to save his life in the same way: he just had to say he was not a Christian. Having witnessed his friends being so willing to die for the name of Jesus, however, singing songs of praise as they went, the man looked at the bodies of his murdered friends and said, "Their God is my God." With that he became the twenty-first martyr.[64]

We started the book by asking a question: "If I really believe what I claim to believe, how then should I live?" In this concluding chapter, we have the answer: "If anyone would come after me, let him deny himself and take up his cross and follow me. For whoever would save his life will lose it, but *whoever loses his life for my sake will find it*" (Matthew 16:24-25, emphasis added). All the implications of faith are summarized in this.

If we really believe that Jesus is the Christ—that he is Lord and Messiah—then we must follow him. If we follow him, it will undoubtedly cost us our life, but it will give us so much more in return. In the Gospel message, God offers us himself so that in him we might have true life.

Trust and surrender is always predicated by God's love for us. We love because he first loved us. We obey because he first set us free from the chains of sin and death. We take up our cross to follow Jesus because he first took up the cross we couldn't bear. It might be scary to consider such a radical surrender of our lives to God, but when we grasp the depths of his perfect love, it is the only thing that makes sense to do.

Christian, I pray that as you have read this book that God through the Holy Spirit has called you to embark with renewed vigor upon the journey of Christian discipleship—the journey of faith. You now stand at a precipice—at a fork in the road. What you do next is up to you. The Lord is beckoning you to follow him—to come and die that you might live. The only question remaining is, "Do you believe?"

CHAPTER 20 NOTES

[56] Daly Focus, "What the media isn't reporting on ISIS' beheading of 21 Christian men," focusonthefamily.com.
https://jimdaly.focusonthefamily.com/what-the-media-isnt-reporting-on-isis-beheading-of-21-christian-men/, (Accessed on August, 1, 2018).

[57] Tacitus, *The Annals and History of Tacitus: A New and Literal English Version*, trans. and ed. D.A. Talboys (D.A. Talboys, London, 1839), pg 362-363.

[58] Tim Dowley, *Introduction to the History of Christianity*, (Fortress Press, Minneapolis, 2013), 104.

[59] Dietrich Bonhoeffer, *The Cost of Discipleship*, (Touchstone, New York, 1995), kindle edition, 1137. Used by permission.

[60] Charles Spurgeon, "Christ is All," Metropolitan Tabernacle Pulpit Volume 17, Sermon #1006—Colossians 3:11.

[61] David Platt, *Radical*, (Multnomah Books, Colorado Springs, 2010), 7. Used by permission.

[62] A.W. Tozer, *Man: The Dwelling Place of God*, (Wing Spread Publishers, Camp Hill, PA, 2008), 68. Used by permission.

63 *Band of Brothers*, "Carentan," Directed by Mikael Salomon. Written by Stephen Ambrose and E. Max Frye. HBO, September 16, 2001.

64Aggie Catholic Blog, "1 of The 21 Men Beheaded Was Not a Christian – Until He Saw The Death of Those Who Refused to Deny Jesus," aggiecatholicblog.org. https://www.aggiecatholicblog.org/2015/03/1-of-the-21-men-beheaded-was-not-a-christian-until-he-saw-the-death-of-those-who-refused-to-deny-jesus/, (Accessed on August 1, 2018).

For this reason I bow my knees before the Father, from whom every family in heaven and on earth is named, that according to the riches of his glory he may grant you to be strengthened with power through his Spirit in your inner being, so that Christ may dwell in your hearts through faith—that you, being rooted and grounded in love, may have strength to comprehend with all the saints what is the breadth and length and height and depth, and to know the love of Christ that surpasses knowledge, that you may be filled with all the fullness of God.

Now to him who is able to do far more abundantly than all that we ask or think, according to the power at work within us, to him be glory in the church and in Christ Jesus throughout all generations, forever and ever. Amen.

—Ephesians 3:14-21

APPENDIX

OUR DEEPEST DESIRE

Note from the author: I first wrote this as an article for a website a few months before starting this book. I desperately wanted to include it in the book because it has been instrumental in my own faith journey, but I couldn't quite get it to fit comfortably as a chapter within any of the sections. It is certainly a direct application of putting on the Belt of Truth, and in many ways, our "fig leaves" are an enemy of faith as God has called us to walk out our faith in community. Nonetheless, it still felt forced to include it in Part IV: Enemies of Faith, so I decided to include it as an appendix. I pray that you will still give it the same time and attention that you have the rest of the book.

The world can be a lonely place. It has been said that our society is the most connected, via technology, and yet the loneliest in the history of time. It is no wonder then that we see so many people deeply hurting—and that depression and suicide are on the rise. We were created for deep, intimate, life-giving relationships, and yet these types of relationships seem to evade us. Why? Is it because of technology? Is it because of social media? While I think these things have amplified the problem, I don't believe they are the root of it. I think the issue is far more sinister, far more destructive, and has been at work far longer, subtly obstructing that which we desire most: to be fully known and loved unconditionally.

The first two chapters of the Bible (Genesis 1-2) tell us we were created to be in intimate relationship with both God and people—naked, free, and unimpeded. But something happens in Genesis 3:

Adam and Eve are seduced into sin by the serpent. In an instant, relationship is broken. The first thing they do after rejecting God's commandment and eating the forbidden fruit is hide from God and cover themselves from each other with fig leaves.

Sin has had the same effect on us. We, too, were created for intimacy. It is our deepest desire to be fully known and loved unconditionally, yet sin has robbed us of this. We believe if we were fully known—with all our sinfulness, brokenness, messiness, and ugliness—we would not be loved. So, we put on a mask—a fig leaf if you will—and we cover the parts we're ashamed of. We present ourselves as the version of us we believe we need to be in order to receive the love we so deeply desire. The love this gets us is not the love we desire, however. We still feel unknown because true intimacy does not exist unless we are fully loved *and* fully known.

Thankfully, Genesis 3 (where Adam and Eve first choose sin) is just the beginning of the story. The rest of the Bible is about a God who so loves those he has created, that he will stop at nothing to provide a way for the broken relationships to be restored. In Jesus Christ, the effects of sin have been destroyed, and the chasm created between God and us has been bridged. We no longer need to hide: "But now in Christ Jesus you who once were far away have been brought near by the blood of Christ.... For through him we...have access to the Father by one Spirit (Ephesians 2:13, 18 NIV)."

So why do Christians still feel lonely? Why was this *my* story? Why did I feel as if no one really knew me? Why was I lonely to the point of a dark depression and a deep despair?

In Exodus, God delivers Israel from slavery in the land of Egypt in a mighty and miraculous way. Yet when they get out into the desert and start to get hungry, they actually want to go back to Egypt! They want to go back to the familiar "comforts" and "security" of their slavery. They were free, but they didn't know how to live like it.

There is a similar truth in our salvation. There is a gap—a logical breakdown even—between what we believe intellectually and how that informs and directs the way we actually live our lives. In order to know God in a way that satisfies our deepest desire, we have to continue to step out in faith, to face our fears, and to confront our own "slave-like mentality." We have to willfully decide to stop hiding from God and to remove our proverbial fig leaves, as scary as that may be.

Our first step is to let the truths of the Gospel give us courage to be painfully honest with ourselves (remember the Belt of Truth). We are completely and entirely known by God, loved unconditionally because of Jesus' death on the cross. If God knows every bad thing we have done and has forgiven us for all those things, then we don't have to hide from him. We don't have to fear being "found out," losing his love, or being abandoned by him. Like the Apostle Paul, we can boast (be brutally honest) in our weaknesses!

The next step is getting to know ourselves. Many of us have become so used to hiding and wearing our masks that we've lost track of who we really are. We've suppressed the things that have hurt us most, and we've become deeply disconnected from understanding what we are feeling and how to communicate that. We no longer know how to be known.

The Gospel and God's grace can become clichés that hang on our bulletin boards but lack any real power in our lives because we don't allow them to permeate our own story. We get the temptation to talk about things from the past as if being a new creation in Christ means we're no longer connected to or influenced by the hurts we have experienced. We oversimplify dealing with buried hurts by saying things like "nail it to the cross" or "Jesus already took care of that." These things are true, but people are more complex than that. Pain still needs to be grieved.

Becoming a Christian doesn't automatically heal all our old wounds. The power is in the fact that it frees us up to be unafraid to confront things we've tried to forget about because they were so painful. It equips us with tools necessary to deal with the hurt so true healing can occur. We are given a Great Counselor in the Holy Spirit, who will seek the depths of our hearts and uncover things we have long run from or forgotten about. He will help us reframe those experiences through the lens of the Gospel, and he will be a comforter to us as we grieve.

As you step out in faith toward Gospel healing, I strongly recommend finding a pastor or counselor you trust to meet with regularly to begin walking through your story and more deeply understand who you are—to understand your wounds, fears, sin struggles, shames, insecurities, passions, gifts, etc. In addition, there are many good books that can help you toward this end. For myself, *The Anatomy of the Soul* by Curt Thompson and *From Bondage to Bonding* by Nancy Groom were incredibly life changing. Paul Tripp also has a number of great resources with a pastoral counseling emphasis.

Furthermore, I strongly recommend a season of solitude (not away from people but away from worldly distractions) where you apply what was discussed in chapter twelve and take a season away from media and entertainment in order to read and prayerfully reflect on your thoughts and feelings. Journaling can be a very helpful exercise.

The one caveat in all this, however, is that while Christian counseling is a wonderful tool in the toolbelt of our Maker, it must remain simply that. The Gospel is the answer, not counseling. Counseling is a way to practically apply the Gospel, but we must never let it trump Biblical truth. Counseling textbooks must never take precedence over the word of God, and we must always remember that we are first a sinner, second sinned against.

This means that while we all have been deeply wounded by others (some in truly horrific ways), and our hurts deserve to be heard, affirmed, and grieved, we must fight the temptation to adopt a "victim mentality." As strange as it sounds, many of us find great comfort and security in the familiarity of being wounded and broken. But if we're not careful, this will create a disposition that inhibits Gospel healing and keeps us in a perpetual state of brokenness. It will inhibit us from taking the necessary ownership and responsibility over our own lives and our actions.

Finally (and this is perhaps the hardest part), we have to take off the fig leaves we are using to hide/protect ourselves from other people. It is not enough to press into our own story, seeking to understand ourselves better—our hurts, fears, and shame. We have to share those things with other believers. We cannot walk out our faith in the duplicity of being known by God while continuing to hide from others.

1 John 4:20 explains the intrinsic link between our relationship with God and our relationship with our brothers and sisters in Christ. Here, John explains that we can't claim we love an invisible God while hating those who are tangible. In a similar fashion, we can't experience intimacy with an invisible God while avoiding it with those who are physically present.

One night as I was in the midst of learning and applying all this in my own life, I was praying, and I cried out to God: "God, I believe that fullness of joy is found in you alone [Psalm 16], but why can't I find it? Why am I still lonely? Why am I still depressed?" In perhaps the clearest response I have ever received from God, he responded (not audibly but just as clear): "Fullness of joy is found in me alone, but you won't find it alone with me. Not because I can't, but because I won't, because I am passionate about my body—the church. I have designed you to be in relationship with other people; it is through them that I make myself manifest. You won't experience a fullness of Me that brings joy and contentment apart from authentic relationships with brothers and sisters in Christ."

God's creational intent for us relationally is two-fold: he has wired us to be fully known and loved unconditionally, by God *and* by others. We have to start letting people (specifically the Christian community) see our messiness—our nakedness—"warts and all." 1 John 1:7 contends, "If we walk in the light, as he is in the light, we have fellowship with one another, and the blood of Jesus his Son cleanses us from all sin." And James 5:16 adds, "Therefore, confess your sins to one another and pray for one another, that you may be healed."

Not everybody will respond with the love, grace, and acceptance of Jesus as we step out in faith by removing the proverbial fig leaves. God does not promise us that by stepping out in faith all things will align perfectly in our lives and we will never experience hurt and disappointment in relationships again. But he does promise us that his love is sufficient to validate and affirm our identity and worth so that we don't need to fear the rejection of some. He also promises us that those who are being led by the Holy Spirit will respond to us with the love, grace, and acceptance of Jesus. We don't get to choose the people God will work through to bring intimate relationship into our lives. We must simply seek to live our lives amongst a community of believers in increasing transparency and authenticity, not seeking to meet our needs, but the needs of those in the community first, and trusting that God will take care of the rest.

God has designed us to experience *his* grace, love, and acceptance through our relationships with other people. It is the way an invisible God becomes tangible in our relationship with him. If we continue to hide from others, we are hiding from God, and we will never experience the type of intimacy for which we are longing. We will be stuck in the vicious cycle of trying to earn love by hiding behind a mask while being desperately lonely because we aren't truly known. We were created to be in authentic, "naked" relationships—to be truly known, and we are freed up to do so by the blood of Jesus.

In response to my prayer, God was calling me to step out in faith relationally. I could no longer wear the mask I was so used to hiding behind. I had to drop the façade and be real, authentic, transparent, vulnerable, messy, and even broken. Yes, it was scary, but as I did this, God met my needs for intimacy in a way that far exceeded anything I had known before. The depression, the anxiety, the cheap substitute for intimacy in the form of a pornography addiction that I had struggled with most of my life—it all began to dissipate, and for the first time, I didn't feel alone.

Learning how to be known will take time and intentionality. It will be scary and requires a lot of faith, but it is worth it. Cling to the truths of the Gospel and be empowered by them to take the necessary steps in faith toward true emotional and relational healing.

A Word of Thanks

It truly takes a village to write a book, and I am exceedingly grateful for the village the Lord has provided me.

First, I want to thank God the Father for his son Jesus Christ, through whom I have been forgiven much. Truly, "the steadfast love of the LORD never ceases; his mercies never come to an end; they are new every morning; great is (his) faithfulness" (Lam. 3:22-23).

I thank my wife for enduring with me through this process. Thank you for having enough faith in the Lord, this project, and me to allow me to see it to completion despite the spiritual, emotional, and financial toll it has taken on us. I am eternally grateful for your love and support.

Third, I want to thank my dear friend, Brandon Scalf, for the on-going support and helpful contributions to chapter one. You are truly like a brother to me. Our many late-night conversations have helped sharpen and mold me in to the man I am today and have enabled me to better articulate this message I am so passionate about.

Next, thank you to my wonderful editors, Donna Ferrier and Laurelen Müller. Your dedication to detail has provided a polish to this final work I never could have achieved without your help.

Finally, this book would have never been possible without the countless people (more than I can list) who have supported me through prayer and financial giving over the past five years. Specifically, thank you to Ted and Andrea (Mom) Taylor, Wes and Joanne Hudson (especially for giving up your space to let us live with you), Brian and Katie Irk, Dennis and Rochelle Meyer, Christian and Melanie Regan, Peter Davis, Tim and Christen Stahl, Andy and Jill Stanton, David and Erin Elliott, Abraham Olivar, Joe Whattoff, and Laura Jones for your financial support throughout the writing process.

*A*BOUT THE *A*UTHOR

Craig Miller lives in Indianapolis, Indiana with his wife, Brittany, where they serve their local church in a lay capacity. He has a MATS (Master of Arts, Theological Studies) from Midwestern Baptist Theological Seminary. Craig also writes and teaches on a voluntary basis for Dead Men Ministries (deadmenstuff.com).

For questions, inquiries, or booking requests, email Craig at craig@deadmenstuff.com.

LITERATURE
RESOURCES FOR REVIVAL

DM Literature is a division of Dead Men Ministries. Dead Men exists to equip disciples of Jesus and grow church leaders.

FOR MORE RESOURCES VISIT:

deadmenstuff.com

Crusade

INVITING REVIVAL

deadmenstuff.com/crusade

22660249R00168

Made in the USA
Lexington, KY
22 December 2018